Additional Praise for Scold's Bridle

Scold's Bridle explores the constraints patriarchy and institutional religion placed on white, Western women from the sixteenth through the twenty-first century through a series of short stories. These stories span five centuries and show how women were often part of these constraints by exploring the experiences and actions of three female archetypes in modern-day Sacramento California, early twentieth-century Pocatello, antebellum Mississippi, colonial Massachusetts, and Reformation Scotland. In all these historical locations, these women take out their trauma on and cooperate with patriarchy and institutional religion to oppress other women, especially their daughters and those younger or more disadvantaged than themselves.

Russell has a real talent for conjuring the historical periods that serve as the setting of her stories. Details and dialogue place the reader in these times and places. Her historical exploration of the limits on women's behavior and their tendency to take both their petty frustrations and need for survival out on other women leads readers to consider their own role in continuing this generational experience. This work is a must read for anyone interested in feminism and gender studies especially in a post-Dobbs v. Jackson world.

—Lindsay J. Starkey, Ph.D., Associate Professor of History
Kent State University

A Hummer-driving preacher's wife whose heart has been corrupted by pedophilia and a lust for money, a pregnant, twentieth-century teen urged by societal dictates into a lukewarm marriage, a different young woman, a century earlier, forced by those same societal dictates into an abortifacient tea before giving her Black slave a cruel public whipping. These are among the two dozen vignettes in *Scold's Bride*, a collection of linked stories that ambitiously seeks to trace white women's choice to align with race over gender, while deftly bringing us to the realization, as we are carried on a swift backward current in time, that the constraints placed on the women in this collection are stubbornly timeless. *Scold's Bridle* announces the auspicious debut of Ronna Russell, whose voice comes to us at an essential time in American feminist literature. The characters in this collection will leave neither one's heart nor one's mind.

—Jacinda Townsend, author of *Trigger Warning*,
Mother Country and *Saint Monkey*

A haunting tale told backwards through time, Russell's collection of short stories held my attention from the first page to the last. With beautiful prose and vibrant characters, Russell weaves a tale that is not only harrowing, and, at times, disturbing, but relatable. Engaging and smart, this is a story that carries a lot of weight and importance. I highly recommend it!

—Amber Garza, author of *In a Quiet Town* and *When I Was You*

Wow! I just this minute finished *Scold's Bridle*—indeed, I couldn't set it down until I had! *Scold's Bridle* is highly ingenious in the way it traces the same characters back through the centuries as they play out variations on their relationships and stories. The common thread is how women survive the patriarchy and the church, or, sadly, how they do not survive it. Though one of the main protagonists, Rebecca, is introduced in the first part of the novel as the predatory and cynical brains behind a church that exploits its congregation, this turns out to be an almost forgivable quid pro quo as we trace her journey back through the centuries in various churches that perpetrate increasingly cruel and unjustified violence to women. The final nail-biting chapters bring to life the unspeakable violence that was, historically, perpetrated against nonconforming women in the name of God.

It's a tough read, and not for the fainthearted, but these things did all happen, and *Scold's Bridle* gives us an up close and personal look into the how and the why—a kind of genealogy of misogyny if you will. In terms of craft, the book is meticulously researched. Every chapter is alive with rich detail—it's hard to imagine that Russell was not actually there, and that these events did not unfold before her observant gaze.

Scold's Bridle is an uncomfortable, uncompromising, gripping account of how religious men have exploited and punished women for the last 400 years.

—Dr. Claire Robson, author of *Writing Beyond Recognition: Queer Restorying for Social Change*

This collection of beautifully written stories swoops from 2015 on America's West Coast all the way across and back—through an enchanting feat of reverse manifest destiny—to medieval Scotland. The strengths of the women (Rebecca, Rae Ann, Delfa) and the weaknesses of our species are on intimate display through these main characters as they highlight humanity's capacity for inhumane treatment of one another—all in fulfillment of others' expectations, borne from the restrains of religion in a patriarchal society. The author's combination of riveting microscopic sensory details and panoramic themes sweep and reverberate through the centuries, to the point where we read the final story at the edge of our seats, at times reading/watching through the gaps in our fingers, partially shielding our eyes. Because of the author's energy, which springs from the page through the careful control of every word, sentence, paragraph, and episode, we're charmed and captivated, upset and empathetic—we want to look away, but can't, from the final acts of bravery in the face of arcane punishment. What a beautifully woven and at times haunting tapestry, this book.

—Bob King, Professor of English
Kent State University

Searing, unflinching, magical: *Scold's Bridle* is a psychic journey of the body, connecting the dots between the white woman's cruel participation in the making of the United States, cellular memory, and a blush of hope for change.

—Anneliese Kamola, author of "Counter Curses"

I have read this book twice and want to read it a third time. I love it. Yes, it has powerful, recurring themes of violence and cruelty, but it is lovely and fascinating, as well. As we learn more about the characters, we come to understand that some of them are doing the best that they can. Their observations, their interiority, teach us more about them, their motives, and about the other characters, too. In Pocatello 1910 Rebecca tells us, "Ma can cook, clean, and fight at the same time." There is humor too, she worries, ". . . Delfa might have lost her mind, and I can't be out here with a crazy person and a dead body." Rebecca and Delfa are preparing that dead body for burial and it's a moment of great tenderness. I cannot stop thinking about it, even weeks later, it's so powerful.

Descriptions involving all the senses—especially sight but also sound, taste, smell, and touch—create a vivid backdrop for the narratives. Several characters experience events with a sixth sense, and this moves the action forward, backward, and sideways, quickly. How water looks, and what it means, are clearly important in each story, as are many other symbols. I wonder about the snakes and the amulets. This is why I need to read it again.

—Dr. Linda Spurlock Ph.D., Associate Professor of Anthropology
Kent State University

A Hummer-driving preacher's wife whose heart has been corrupted by pedophilia and a lust for money, a pregnant, twentieth-century teen urged by societal dictates into a lukewarm marriage, a different young woman, a century earlier, forced by those same societal dictates into an abortifacient tea before giving her Black slave a cruel public whipping. These are among the two dozen vignettes in Scold's Bride, a collection of linked stories that ambitiously seeks to trace white women's choice to align with race over gender, while deftly bringing us to the realization, as we are carried on a swift backwards current in time, that the constraints placed on the women in this collection are stubbornly timeless. Scold's Bridle announces the auspicious debut of Ronna Russell, whose voice comes to us at an essential time in American feminist literature. The characters in this collection will leave neither one's heart nor one's mind.

—Jacinda Townsend, Assistant Professor of Literary Arts
Brown University

Scold's Bridle

Ronna Russell

Ronna Russell

Sidekick Press
Bellingham, Washington

Publisher's Note: This is a work of fiction. Names, characters, places, and incidents are a product of the author's imagination. Locales and public names are sometimes used for atmospheric purposes. Any resemblance to actual people, living or dead, or to businesses, companies, events, institutions, or locales is completely coincidental.

Published 2024
Printed in the United States of America
ISBN: 978-1-958808-23-8
LCCN: 2023921600

Sidekick Press
2950 Newmarket Street, Suite 101-329
Bellingham, Washington 98226
sidekickpress.com

Scold's Bridle

Cover design by Andrea Gabriel
Cover art by Ken Miller

CONTENTS

Author's Note

Time isn't linear, they say. The past, present, and future exist simultaneously like slices in a loaf of bread. We visit the past through memory or meditation, yet time only flows forward, and all we inhabit is the present, fleeting moment. We are cosmic beings experiencing reality in a corporeal body as an extension of our psychic self. Or something like that. We are who we have always been, entangled with our ancestors' DNA and stardust.

Scold's Bridle is a collection of stories on the culture of white women throughout modern history. Who are we and how did we become ourselves? When did we begin choosing the social construct of race over that of gender? These stories are each set in a different time and place, beginning in the twenty-first century and ending in the sixteenth, moving backward through time and visiting the same characters as they were during an earlier time and in a previous place. These stories are based on true events seen through the eyes of the main characters during fleeting moments of their participation in these events.

While researching the writing of these stories, I consistently encountered women either being subjected to or subjecting others to a horrifying level of cruelty—even when I wasn't looking for it. Anthropological studies taught me that epigenetics and intergenerational trauma are vastly entangled and mysterious. Through history and women's studies, I've found that the past does not represent what we are told, and at every turn, religion holds the sharp stick, the torch, or the bridle. Violence is quite literally in our DNA, imprinted in a fully formed ovum at birth.

From my own experiences, I know my ancestral mothers and their children suffered, mostly in silence, and passed that suffering and silence on as a curse, even while vowing to do better. I failed my children in ways I never thought I would and came through for them in ways they will never know. As I wrote this book, I began to wonder if, perhaps, we can visit our brutal past selves and gather them to us, so that our future can be a gentler place.

—Ronna Russell

Story One:
Sacramento 2015

Rebecca

As usual, I make an entrance at the last minute, and settle into my place at the far end of the first row on the right. I angle my hips into the blood-red weave of the padded pew and scan the sanctuary, twisting my upgraded wedding rings. This position provides me with a 180-degree view, starting with my husband, Brother Leon Wolfe, behind the pulpit and then heading all the way to the back where the reprobates sit. I can see who is there and who isn't, who comes in late, and who slips out early. *Packed house tonight, even the balcony is full.* And the teenagers on the far side: who's hunting who.

Speaking of teenagers, my sixteen-year-old daughter Rae Ann is sitting by Tony, the all-star football player from the high school. She's smooshed up against him and giggling. Tony's dimple deepens below his angled, bronze cheekbone. I can't blame her; none of these pansy church boys ever build a muscle. And he is beautiful. Rae Ann surreptitiously strokes Tony's bicep with her fingertips, and I imagine how he feels. I bought him that Eton button-down just to watch it spread like butter over his carved shoulders. That boy stops my heart. I know it's nuts, but I'm closer in age to him than I am to Leon. Tony flexes under Rae

Ann's fingers, and she sees me watching. I flash her one perfectly sculpted, raised eyebrow, sharp as a switchblade—it cuts into her and her smile fumbles. *Gonna have to shut that down. Rae Ann is just a baby. But Tony . . . Tony is grown.*

I turn back to the front to see Brother Charles, the organist, staring at Tony too, his full lips practically hanging open. *God, it figures.* Brother Charles has The Struggle. When he glances at me, I give him a half brow and a stern Rouge Coco in Deep Red smirk, and his cheeks blanch dead white underneath his carefully crafted five-o'clock shadow.

God can't heal what you won't confess, Brother Charles. Brother Charles's fiancée is pure as the driven. Maybe her love will heal him, I believe God can do that. But Brother Charles is probably not the best choice to lead Pray Away Support Group.

The choir members rustle to their feet and softly begin to sing *I Surrender All* while the EasyTithe app instructions bloom behind the pulpit on the custom PixelFLEX LED screen. It's more technology than we can afford, but you have to spend money to make money, as they say. Our new Church of the Third Angel™ motion graphic shrinks to the upper left corner, the fluttering of the angel's wings shedding sparkles of light across the screen. Behind "Three Simple Steps to Giving," soft background images scroll: hungry-looking brown babies, sweating missionaries under thatched roofs, "Life Is a Gift from God" protest signs, little white children with their hands folded in prayer, a bloody crown of thorns, the American flag—*yes, Jesus*—and Leon shaking hands with the mayor and the chief of police. Then, a flash screen of "ENROLL NOW! Miracles Academy™ starts soon!" and "2 Corinthians 9:7" runs on the ticker at the bottom of the screen: "Give what you have decided in your heart to give, for God loves a cheerful giver! Receive Extra Blessings and Extra Savings when you click to add Brother Leon Wolfe's NEW book, *Those Who Seek Him* for only $24.99! Monthly Prayers for You™ Membership FREE with purchase!'"

The IT guy has outdone himself again, and my heart is overjoyed to see this miracle of technological art in Jesus' name. *It's all for the glory of God. I believe that.* Tonight's service is the start of a big revival push to take Church of the Third Angel to the next level. Leon would never do this on his own—that man would be happy driving his ancient rattletrap Oldsmobile and ministering to the same twenty-five people for the rest of his goddamn life while we try to survive on their pocket change. New churches are being seeded all over the place, and I ain't gonna sit here while we dwindle down to nothing. Not while Abundance Temple in the city lures our youth group away with their light shows and rock stars. Last year, they got Justin *fucking* Bieber, and now they have a Holy Beans coffee shop franchise in the goddamn lobby. They used to call us a sister church, but now they're filching our people. It's enough already. They don't know who they're dealing with. I am going to give them a run for their money, and they taught me how to do it in their very own overpriced seminars. People need Jesus, and I intend to make him easy to find.

I sneak a peek at my phone to see dollar amounts tick-tick-ticking up on the EasyTithe tracker as donations roll in while the old-school wooden offering plates pass up and down the pews, essential for siphoning cash from the old people who don't use cell phones. We have a few leftover members from the old days who haven't died off yet, but they are always up for an antiabortion protest, and some have deep pockets. I keep a sharp eye on the ushers passing the plates; sometimes bills accidentally jump into their trouser pockets. The plates are loaded as the ushers carry them out in teetering stacks. EasyTithe flashes me a record intake alert, so I flip my phone upside down in the side pocket of my Chloé bag, inhaling a whiff of leather. *Praise Jesus, that Hummer ain't gonna pay for itself.*

I smile up at the IT guy in the sound booth. None of this is possible without him, so we pay him well, even though he isn't even a Christian. He runs the music, security, and all the social media. Discretion is part of his job, but just in case, I had Tony plant a baggie of coke, just enough for felony distribution, and a USB of child porn under the passenger seat of his Honda Civic. That shit ain't as hard to come by as you would think. The porn, I mean. The coke was mine. A little extra perk never hurt anyone and, Lord knows, I've got a lot going on. And with a bought-and-paid-for K9 unit on speed dial, we are all set to keep the IT guy in line. A twenty-five-thousand-dollar donation to the police department goes a long way in a small town. I never told Tony what was in that package he planted, and he never asked. He loves doing odd jobs for me and is always sniffing around. I don't want to scare him off.

Leon strides to the pulpit with heavy steps, slumped shoulders straining in his frayed suit jacket. The screen fades to a silhouette of Calvary, backlit by a cloudscape-sunbeam montage as the angel weeps in the corner.

"Blessed are they who hunger and thirst after righteousness for THEY. SHALL. BE. FILLED! Let Jesus fill you up tonight! Are you ready for SALVATION? Are you ready for HEALING? ARE YOU READY FOR REVIVAL?" Leon's voice thunders.

"Hallelujah, Brother Wolfe," I holler back, clapping my hands. I always call him "Brother Wolfe." He likes it, makes him swell. Which I can see is happening because he heard me. He never could resist me. Brother Charles fingers the organ softly, building a suspenseful beat. He bounces on the organ bench, silky black hair slipping forward.

"Yes, Lord. Preach!" come calls from the congregation. They're feeling the Spirit. I'm feeling it too, because Leon's voice begins to rasp as he gets going. My knees tighten under my Ted Baker skirt. I slide my hands over the ombre silk pleats and squeeze my thighs together, digging the spike heel of my Sophia Webster into the carpet. Leon's voice has always thrummed me like a harp and still does. Brother Charles picks up the tempo and nods to Sister Sarah in the choir loft. She steps to the microphone and begins a low hum to match Brother Charles's notes. Perfect harmony. Those two have this down to a science.

"Are you ready to sing, Sister Sarah?" Leon smiles in her direction.

"Yes, Brother Wolfe," she sings back. She never misses a beat. Or a counseling session with my husband.

I look right through her plain face, plush breasts straining against polyester lace, platinum hair wound around her head in a floppy bun. I remember how it tumbled down over Leon's thick hands in his office. That security camera the IT guy installed for me works in several ways. My throat constricts at the memory. It hurt me to see them together, but I can't blame Leon for giving in to temptations of the flesh. The pressures of growing this church for the Lord are many, and he's always had a weak spirit. He never stood a chance once Sister Sarah moved on him. It's almost funny how fast he gave in. God knows that's how I came to be here. He would never have married me if I hadn't gotten pregnant with Rae Ann at seventeen. We both have our needs, and we're in too deep to let them get in the way now.

Sister Sarah croons her clear soprano into the mic. "Oooh, He's coming back just like He said He would." Brother Charles harmonizes with some backup vocals in his smooth baritone, "Just like He said He would."

"Praise the Lord," Leon calls out as he paces the platform, sweat beading in his forehead crevices beneath his damp, frazzled mess of a comb-over. *Jesus, he looks old.* Sometimes I forget he has twenty years on me. He slides off his suit jacket and pulls his handkerchief from his back pocket. Sister Sarah moves her ever-so-slightly rounded hips to the music as the other musicians join in on guitar, bass, and drums.

The congregation rises, one by one, singing, clapping, and swaying to the music. I stand along with them, eyes closed, waving my hands in the air, that fresh candy apple mani sparkling alongside the dime-sized rocks on my fingers. It's no good for the First Lady of the church to be dowdy. Fuck that. You have to set yourself apart. Also, Leon likes the red. I peek around. *This is good; they're all on their feet. Tonight is the night. Has to be.*

"Make love to Jesus!" Leon urges, raising his hands overhead, which pulls his padded vest across his paunch. *Doesn't look weird unless you know.* The rising sound of worship comes in waves. *God is here. Yes, Lord. I prayed on this, God told me He would be here tonight and here He is.* When the music sweeps everyone away, you can feel His presence. God called Brother Leon Wolfe to serve. He is the arbiter of the way, the truth, and the life, so everything we do must be right. What could matter more than saving souls from Hell? It's the ultimate battle against Satan himself. *I believe that.*

Leon is really winding up the crowd, pleading now, "Come to Jesus tonight, before it's too late. Hear His cry for your soul. God is right here with us. Seek Him. He is waiting for you." The worshippers moan.

Brother Charles and Sister Sarah turn up the volume. She whips out her tambourine, keeping the beat against the increasing sway of those delicious hips. Brother Charles nods to the choir and they join in.

> But when you hear that trumpet sound
> That's when the dead in Christ shall rise
> In the twinkling of an eye
> We shall meet Him in the sky

The congregation is in a frenzy now, dancing around in the aisles. I join in, speaking in tongues for good measure, but not straying too far from my seat. If I start out loud, the language just comes, and then I am a conduit for the Holy Spirit, falling right into Jesus' arms as He speaks right through me. Leon stops his pacing at the top of the platform stairs on my side. I sidestep back to my place. Our eyes meet for a moment. He gives a pump-it-up wave to Brother Charles and then reaches into his pocket.

Here it comes. I close my eyes.

Jesus, Jesus, Jesus.

A deafening boom fills the sanctuary, followed by a sharp crack. Vibration hits my chest and tingles through my limbs. Leon stumbles backward magnificently, catching himself on the corner of the organ. The congregation gasps as one; the sound of ringing electronics hangs in the air. The wooden pulpit is split completely in half, burnt wires smoking and splinters littering the carpet. Pieces of pulpit splay out like a sacrifice. Silence falls over the worshippers.

"HALLELUJAH," Leon bellows.

"JESUS!" I scream, right on cue, and begin speaking in tongues again, "HONDALEE, HONDALEE, SHAKAKA-LAKA."

Leon grabs Sister Sarah's microphone and shouts, "JESUS IS HERE! HALLELUJAH." He resumes pacing the platform.

"Well, if that's not a sign from God, I don't know what is. God just reminded us of His ALMIGHTY POWER."

A pencil-sized shard of pulpit had pierced his shirt sleeve, and a stain of blood spreads through the cheap white cotton, but the tactical gear under his vest had done its job. *Perfect. Couldn't have planned it better. That's the Lord at work right there.*

"I want all the Healers who marched around the hospital walls with us last night to come forward. Come on down, Healers. Let's make a worship tunnel right now, a Holy Fire Tunnel for Jesus. Praise the Lord."

Sister Delfa hoists herself to her feet and waddles down to the altar, the clunky, handmade serpent amulet she always wears swinging back and forth across her bosom, the Healers Team close behind. They line up across the front of the sanctuary facing one another, team members waving banners of red, white, and blue at the entrance and exit of the tunnel. The screen angel's wings shed bursts of flames. I give Sister Delfa a nod of approval for positioning her team in less than a minute. Before service, I'd pulled her aside for personal prayer. I'd told her I knew something special was going to happen tonight because I could feel an unrest in the Spirit. Her beady little eyes lit up bright green just like the snake on her chest, practically shooting out lightning bolts. That's all she needed to get her radar tuned. We can always count on Sister Delfa.

"We hear every day how Satan has us living in fear. Afraid to leave our homes, afraid to gather together. He WANTS us to live in fear. Darkness has descended upon our great land. But I am here to tell you that we are covered by the blood of Jesus! Satan cannot touch you! God is more powerful than any temptation," Leon shouts, tendrils of smoke from the fractured pulpit rising around him. "If you're living in fear tonight, come down here and let Jesus release you from the darkness of the world. Let your spirit rise to meet him with the faith of Abraham. Plead the blood and let him cover you with His divine protection."

The weeping congregation flows forward toward the tunnel. The Healers lay their hands on the worshippers' heads, grasping their raised arms and praying urgently for the release of their bound spirits. Overcome, some tunnel worshippers have to be held up by the elbows and moved along like they are on a spiritual conveyor belt. By the time the throng reaches the exit, most are incoherent in Jesus.

Sister Delfa waits at the exit to the tunnel, pulling people forward and putting her hands on their skin. If anyone she touches has a sickness or a perversion, she can feel it, smell it, sense it. She is in rare form tonight, casting out demons and illnesses right and left. *I have seen God heal the blind and the deaf through her hands. Seen it with my own eyes. Sister Delfa could pray the Devil right out of Hell, her faith is that great.*

This is going to go on for hours. Worshippers are staggering around to the end of the line to go through the tunnel again. The choir is in disarray, but the musicians are keeping it together. Brother Charles dials the organ down and Sister Sarah is . . . sitting in Leon's chair on the platform as if she belongs there. He is pacing more slowly, back and forth, back and forth, praying loudly. I don't see Rae Ann and Tony in the crowd. They're gone. *Damn it.*

I slip out the side door to the church office where the secretary has the deposit ready and waiting. I give the stacks of bills a cursory flip-through. It's annoying to have to deal with cash because you can't get any data. But it is useful. I take a stack of twenties, pull out my safe key, dump the remaining bills inside, and lock it up. I step around the secretary, who is also a pain in the ass but useful, and log into EasyTithe with my encrypted password to verify the night's donations. *Huge numbers. Huge.* This revival kick-off was inspired. Praise services every night for a week, and then Miracles Academy starts. We are running a full-time class schedule for the first time ever. If the Spirit keeps moving like it did tonight, we'll fill every spot. Just think how many Healers we'll ordain and how many souls will be saved. These numbers will put us on the map.

I click on the motion sensor to the camera in Leon's office, log all the way out, and lock the desktop. I peel a few twenties off my stack, slide them into the side pocket of the secretary's faux leather TJ Maxx-looking purse, and leave her to close up the office. I don't know how much she notices, but a little green goodwill can't hurt. Maybe she will find her way to the Coach outlet.

I head back up the hallway to the stairwell behind the platform, which leads to the baptismal tank overlooking the choir loft and sanctuary. No one is in the hall, so I step quickly through the stairwell door and slide the bolt behind me, fingers suddenly trembling. I stand at the bottom of the dank wooden staircase for a moment. My thighs clench. Tony is supposed to be turning the water heater on and laying out robes and towels for the baptisms that are sure to come. I told him to wait for me there. God, I hope he ditched Rae Ann first. If he didn't, I guess I'll know I have misread the situation.

I tiptoe up the unlit stairs, heart pounding and breath catching in my throat, into the waft of chlorine and dim glow emanating from the Purification Chamber above. Muffled hymns seep through the crimson velvet curtains that separate the baptism chamber from the sanctuary. The music seems far away. I reach the top of the stairs and step into the chamber, knees wobbling. Refracted light from the tank's submersible lamp ricochets through the crystal-clear water, filling the chamber with a wavering shimmer. Tony is there, slim hips against the metal handrail, awash in rippling light. Waiting for me with his arms crossed, dark underneath the white of his shirt sleeves.

Jesus.

Rae Ann

So, I'm hiding in the changing room of the Purification Chamber, where I always go when church gets crazy. There is nowhere else to get away from the noise. If anyone finds me, I'll just pretend I'm here to help sinners get ready to be baptized. That would be a good pastor's daughter thing to do, actually. If I stay in the sanctuary, I can't just sit on the pew and not pray or anything. Mom will notice and snipe at me about setting a good example. All she cares about is appearances these days. I don't even remember the last time we had an actual conversation.

And if I get too close to the Fire Tunnel, I'm afraid Sister Delfa will grab me and shove me in. That whole tunnel thing weirds me out. I kind of want to be part of everything going on, but the emotional wave everyone else is feeling escapes me. When they're all weeping and speaking in tongues, I just feel numb. This crazy energy sweeps through the congregation and it's like I have shields up. I'm not sure if I wish I didn't have shields so I could feel the group vibe or if I'm glad about the protection.

Sometimes I kneel at the altar, put my head down, and close my eyes just to shut it all out. I let my mind go and the noise around me gets softer. I imagine a cocoon wrapping around me, muffling out the sounds. Somewhere in my head, I know when it's time to get up, and I pretend I was praying the whole time. But hiding in the changing room is way better. I can barely hear the music from the sanctuary in here, but from the sound of it the Fire Tunnel is still going strong. Service won't be over for a while, so I curl up on a stack of towels to wait it out, rubbing the terry cloth between my fingers.

Church didn't used to be this nuts. When I was a kid, the congregation was pretty small, and a lot of older people treated me like a little princess. It was like having a bunch of super nice grandparents, which was great because my own grandparents were pretty strict. Grandpa was the pastor here before Dad, but now he has dementia, and Grandma died a few years ago. Back then, there was Sunday school and snacks and Bible stories. Mom and Dad drove an old white Oldsmobile and didn't care about money. Like, their main thing was spreading the Gospel.

But maybe salvation was just Dad's thing and not really Mom's because she started complaining about never having any money and then shopping anyway. And then Dad would freak out about the credit card bills. I know Mom was super young when they got married—barely older than I am now, so I guess she never really had any fun. By the time she was eighteen, she was a mom and a preacher's wife. She grew up really poor, the youngest of a bunch of kids. Some of them had already left home by the time she was born. As far as we know, her family all still live out in the boonies in Idaho somewhere. We never see them, not even on holidays. Mom doesn't want to admit her family are kind of hillbillies. I guess she married Dad to get away from them, and being a preacher's wife looked like a nice life—with a real house and food on the table—even though he was way older. But then she got bored. And tired of never going on vacations or having a nice car.

No way Dad was ever going to get a raise or anything, like he would in a regular job. It wasn't enough for Mom anymore.

After Dad took over the church from Grandpa, they started going to these seminars at Abundance Temple about how to grow your church. Then all these visiting evangelists started coming here to hold revivals and preaching about faith healing and miracles and Hell. Mom and Dad changed the name to Church of the Third Angel, and even started advertising on TV and using social media and stuff. Mom was all excited to be in the commercials and got a new wardrobe and a makeover, including a boob job. She lost a bunch of weight too. She even made Dad get new suits, but he never wears them. I can tell she loves the attention, and to be fair, she's still really pretty. I never realized before how much younger than Dad she is. I think all these changes are mainly her idea, but he won't ever tell her no. Mom has a way of getting what she wants.

After their media blitz, tons of new people started coming to our church and we moved into this ginormous house in a gated community. You actually need a code to get in. Don't get me wrong, it's very cool, but I kind of miss our old neighborhood where we knew everyone. I'm there by myself most of the time, just rattling around alone. And now Mom is always talking about how success is a blessing. Like, if God loves you and you're working for him, why wouldn't he want you to have money? Makes sense, I guess.

They sent Tony's mom, Sister Delfa, to Healers' training at Abundance Temple and she came back all creepy and weird. She's the one who started the whole Fire Tunnel thing and is the main teacher at Miracles Academy. Mom says that the more Healers and missionaries we train, the more people will come to church and the more souls will be saved. Like, when people see miracles performed, then they see the power of God and believe. And then they will go to Heaven. And the church makes more money too. So . . . win, win.

One of the new church members, this girl who was practically blind, got healed and didn't even need her glasses anymore. Her eyesight was totally fine after Sister Delfa prayed for her. But then I saw that same girl at Target a week later and she was wearing her glasses again, so I don't know. I tried asking Mom about it, but she said not having faith is a sin and asking the question means I don't have faith. So then I asked her, "What about Abraham and Isaac? If God told you to sacrifice me, would you do it?" And she told me sacrifice was an Old Testament thing and wouldn't happen nowadays. She didn't say no, though.

I shift around on the stack of towels and stretch my tingling legs. I roll the back of my head against the wall and burrow my tailbone into the cheap white terry cloth. Service is still going strong out there while I am trying to figure faith out without asking questions, alone in the dark.

Like I'm thinking about last night, when Sister Delfa and the Healers held a rally at the hospital because of this woman who collapsed on the sidewalk outside Starbucks earlier in the afternoon. See, the Healers were coming out of Starbucks just as the woman basically fainted right in front of them. They were totally sure God made it happen because it was a perfect opportunity for public healing. So they gathered around to pray for her right there on the sidewalk, kneeling down and putting their hands on her. I guess she was having trouble breathing, though, and they thought maybe it was heatstroke because it was about 110 degrees. But, turns out it was actually a heart attack, and someone called 911. No one knows who called, but the Healers were really pissed off. I missed the whole thing, as usual.

After the ambulance took the woman away, Sister Delfa called an emergency prayer meeting at the hospital. By the time I heard about it, a bunch of people had already marched into the hospital to pray outside the ICU, but they got kicked out. Too much noise, I guess. I went down there because I figured Tony would be there with his mom. She always makes him go to everything unless he has football practice, and I knew he didn't. But I couldn't find him anywhere. Anyway, I got to the hospital just as everyone was coming back out. They were all standing around wondering what to do. Dad was already there and started leading the crowd in a song. Dad actually has a great voice, really deep and low. He always used to sing me to sleep when I was little.

We were standing right in the emergency lane. We all had our eyes closed and hands up, singing and praying really hard for this woman to be healed, when somebody came out of the hospital and whispered to Sister Delfa. And Sister Delfa started shaking all over. That's always the sign a message from God is coming— she kind of jerks around before she prophesies, like she is getting her own personal transmission signal. One time, when she started jerking around in church, I whispered, "Beep, beep, red alert," to Tony, but he didn't laugh.

Sister Delfa stepped up onto the curb, trembling all over, her fake red hair coming loose from its cotton candy bun. She said the lady died—I can't remember her name—anyway, she's dead, and Sister Delfa says God told her to raise the woman up because Satan took her too soon. So I guess the plan was we were gonna march around until she woke up from the dead, and the whole crowd followed Sister Delfa over the curb onto the grass. I mean, I guess people can be raised from the dead—Jesus did it in the Bible. But it doesn't seem like the kind of thing that happens nowadays, like sacrificing people. I don't know. I guess that's where faith comes in.

Dad was still at the front of the crowd, and I couldn't get his attention, so I trailed along at the back watching for Tony, but he never came. Mom didn't, either. She's usually always here for this stuff; it's basically her job to show up. I followed the group as we all filed past the brick walls of the hospital. Clumps of wet grass were sticking to my flip-flops and my feet were soaking, but at least the sprinklers turned off. I love the smell of fresh-cut grass, though. The sun had just gone down, and the streetlights were coming on, giving the white satin angel wings on the back of the Healers' T-shirts a weird orange glow.

The Healers started a chant that surged down the line, their voices rising and falling. It reminded me of being at a football game when the wave goes around the stadium. We marched past the doctors' parking lot full of Mercedes, past a dumpster pen, past the open door of the kitchens where employees in hairnets and white aprons leaned against the wall having a smoke break. I was the last one to pass them and I heard their snickers. "Fucking freaks," one of them muttered as the others cracked up. I pretended not to hear.

We made a full loop around the hospital, chanting and praying, which took forever. Hospitals are bigger than you think, and we had to climb over a retaining wall. I had to pee so badly by then. Like, I don't think anyone really thought this through.

Sister Delfa finally stopped us back where we started in the wet grass under the streetlamps. She told us all to put our hands on the hospital walls and plead the blood of Jesus to raise what's-her-name from the dead. I stepped up to the wall beside the others and put my hands on the bricks, still warm from the sun. Silky red dust coated my palms and itched my nose. I closed my eyes and rested my forehead against the wall, listening to the prayers surrounding me. *Can this really work? Can a person actually come back to life?* I know Jesus did after three days, but he was Jesus. I wondered if this lady saw the tunnel of light and if she would come back through it. Maybe she will be bummed to be brought back. Maybe it would be super weird to always be the person who was brought back from the dead for the rest of her life. Just think of all the interviews she would have to do. I would hate that.

After about ten minutes of leaning into the hospital wall, the bricks were cooling down and the prayers were sort of tapering off. That's when the cops showed up. They asked who was in charge and Dad stepped forward. All the cops know who he is, so they were apologetic and said they'd had some complaints and asked if we would take our prayer meeting elsewhere. Dad said, "No problem." I think he was okay with leaving. But someone yelled, "It's public property!" in a confrontational way. Then Dad and the cop kind of nodded to each other, and everyone started wandering over to the parking lot. I heard someone say that we could march up and down the sidewalk, but more people wanted to go for coffee. Like, standing around with no miracles happening made you start to feel a little bit defeated. Maybe it was that lady's time to go and she wasn't coming back. God doesn't always answer prayers.

Sister Delfa was hugging everyone, her pancake makeup that never matched her skin rubbing off on their angel wing shirts. The Healers were practically standing in line for a turn. Her hugs made you feel like you were the only person in the world. People couldn't get enough of her, but I didn't want to get too close. I was afraid she would be able to read my mind or something.

Like, I didn't want her to know that me and Tony went to a party with a bunch of his football buddies and that they were all drinking a lot. I was too scared to drink anything because I knew Dad would wait up for me, so I was the only sober person there. Sometimes, being in the middle of church services feels the same way. Even though Tony was pretty drunk, we talked for a long time and we kissed a lot that night. So I thought that he, like, *liked* me. But that was over a month ago now.

Anyway, Tony is weird lately. He takes forever to text back and never wants to hang out anymore. And then, when the pulpit exploded in the middle of service tonight, he didn't even jump. I practically peed my pants, but he wasn't even surprised. I can't figure out what happened. Why would God explode the pulpit? Dad was bleeding and everything. If God hurt Dad just to make a point, then I am going to be really upset. Like, destruction of property is not even necessary and what is the point? But how else could it have happened? Pulpits don't just explode. Maybe the electronics went haywire or something. But then, everyone started to go up to the Fire Tunnel like they felt the power of God in the explosion, and since I don't feel it, I just have to trust that they know.

Afterward, Tony said he was going to the bathroom and then he never came back. I feel like Mom is getting to him somehow, but maybe I'm just being paranoid. She talks about him all the time and always has him doing chores for her at the church. And after we went to that party, she said something about how she wonders if Tony and his football buddies drink. There's no way she knew about that. She doesn't even know we went out. Does she? But every time I talk to him at church, she is watching. After I got home from that football party, on time and everything, she wasn't even there. Neither was Dad. I feel like something is going on, but I don't know what.

It's gotten dark and quiet all of a sudden in the Purification Chamber changing room. I can breathe, even though the chlorine fumes are pretty strong. My legs are starting to go numb from sitting cross-legged on the towels. I stretch them out, straining to hear the music. You can tell if the tunnel is winding down when Brother Charles starts playing old-time, come-to-Jesus hymns. That means people will be praying through to salvation and wanting to be baptized. I should probably get out of here. I have to pee, anyway. As usual. I slowly open the changing room door and stop when I hear a creak and then a shuffle.

Shit, someone is here.

I peek through the crack in the door as Tony steps into the chamber. I start to say hi and then stop. *What is he doing up here?* I pull back as far behind the door as I can and watch him. He flips the heat switch on the control panel and leans over to touch the water. *Since when is Tony in charge of the baptism tank? He never told me that.*

What the heck? What is he doing?

Tony rubs the back of his neck the way he does when he is nervous. He looks around like he isn't sure what to do next, and then we both hear it—footsteps on the stairs. I freeze as Tony's head jerks toward the staircase. He chews his lower lip, rubs his neck again, and then leans against the metal handrail leading to the tank. He crosses his arms and poses. I can tell he's trying to look cool. The door to the chamber opens and someone steps in. I shift to see who it is, holding my breath. The unmistakable figure of my mother emerges from the shadows. Wavering light casts bright patterns across her face, revealing an expression I have never seen before.

What the heck is going on? What is she doing up here? I can't see Tony's face, but he hunches his shoulders a little as Mom walks toward him like she's in a trance. *She knew he was up here. He knew she was coming.* I can't feel my legs. My hands are numb on the wooden door. Mom steps closer to Tony. I can't hear what she says, but then she puts her hands on his arms and pulls them around her waist. She steps between his legs. She is touching his face and kissing his lips. He kisses her back. Hard.

I can't breathe. I can't move.

I squeeze my eyes closed. This can't be happening. I stand in the darkness. Maybe it's a misunderstanding, and maybe Mom is praying with Tony or something, or I didn't just see what I think I saw.

Eyes open.

Oh, God.

Eyes closed.

My stomach roils. A red film descends behind my eyes. My nostrils flare and my jaw tightens. My tongue goes numb. A clench of rage twists through my chest, my abdomen, my pelvis. My legs tremble to hold it all.

Fuck it.

I slam the changing room door open. The accusation I intend to hurl aborts in my throat at the scene before me, and I run to the curtains, fumbling to find the pull cord within the folds of musty red velvet. I grab the gilt tassels and yank. The heavy drapes separate with a swoosh.

The Fire Tunnel crowd continues their worship, not noticing that the music halted as Brother Charles's hands poise, midair, above the organ keys. I can see Sister Sarah looking over her shoulder, a grin tugging the corner of her mouth, her eyes bright, and Dad's mouth dropping open, his hands drifting by his sides. Their eyes are on the baptism where Mom stands between Tony's thighs. Mom, ever the quick thinker, slaps her hand down on

Tony's forehead, grabs his hand, and raises it above his head in one motion. She closes her eyes, throws her head back, and starts speaking in tongues, pretending like she was praying for Tony the whole time.

I stand behind the curtain as Mom announces to anyone listening that Tony is ready to be baptized. Then she goes back to speaking in tongues and waving her arms around. Tony keeps his eyes closed and pretends to pray with his head bowed, rubbing his fingers over his forehead. I turn back to meet Dad's gaze with a furious glare. *Is he buying this?* The Healers and the congregation have turned toward the front. Dad raises his hands and yells, "Hallelujah!" and Sister Delfa calls out, "Praise the Lord!" and the congregation echoes their words. I uncurl my cramped fingers from the frayed gold tassels of the pull cord, my palms sticky with grime and sweat. I descend the staircase on wobbling legs, slide the bolt free, and run.

I run out of the church to my car, sandals slapping the asphalt, dry summer heat stifling my lungs as I gasp for air. Fumble in my skirt pocket for my keys, drop them twice before I get the car door open. Sweating and shaking in the driver's seat, heart pounding. Turn the engine on, pull out, brake. I ease my car out into the street, forcing myself to go slow. *Be careful.* I rumble out past the streetlights, past the turn onto Greenback Lane, past the old neighborhoods, and into the night.

I drive. I do not know where I am going.

Mom and Tony. Mom and Tony. Mom and Tony.

Most of a tank of gas later, I pull into the gravel parking lot of a trailhead and turn off the car. Turn off the headlights. I cannot see anything at first. I roll down the window and a gust of slightly cooler air drifts across my face. I don't have enough gas to get home and I still have to pee. Moonlight casts a dim glow on the white plastic roof of a port-a-potty by the trailhead map. I climb, wobbly-legged, out of the car and stagger a few steps toward it, blood slowly rushing back into my limbs. I double-check my pocket for my phone, lock the car, and then unlock it in case I need to get back in a hurry. I imagine serial killers lurking behind the trees.

My sandals slide around on the loose gravel of the parking lot as I hurry toward the port-a-potty. I hook a curled knuckle under the outhouse handle and pull, aiming for minimal contact. Door hinges squeak and the acrid stench burns my nostrils. It is pitch black inside. Before stepping in, I press my phone flashlight, inspecting the area around the toilet seat. *Bits of paper on the floor and dried-up pee spots, but nothing too gross.* The door bangs shut behind me, and I swipe a piece of toilet paper to lift the lid with two fingers, holding my phone in my left hand. I avoid shining my flashlight into the toilet. *What crawls around in port-a-potties at night? Rats? Spiders, maybe?* Quick look: all clear, except for the floaters. I slip my phone into my pocket and hold my skirt up high, making sure my keys and phone don't fall into the tank. *That's all I need.* Hold my breath. Careful shifting and lots of hand sanitizer later, I am back in my car.

What now?

I lean my seat back, hearing only insect song.

Mom and Tony.

No wonder he won't talk to me. How long has this been going on? How could she? *This is disgusting. And, oh my God, probably not even legal. I don't understand. I don't understand.* White noise fills my brain as it begins to shut off. I close my eyes. Shimmering blue-and white-light hexagons swim around on the inside of my eyelids, shrinking and expanding, then dissipating into a starfield of cobalt blue dots.

I must have dozed off, because I wake up to tires crunching on the gravel and headlights sweeping through my back window as a car pulls in beside me. *Dad. I forgot to turn off my phone's locator.* As he lumbers toward my car, I am not sure if I am relieved or afraid.

He opens my driver's door and I can tell from the look on his face that he isn't mad, just worried.

"Come on, Rae Ann. Come home. You're just overreacting," he says.

Overreacting? But . . . Mom and Tony!

"We'll come back tomorrow for your car. Come on now."

I get out and close the door behind me, lock it, and then deposit my keys into his outstretched hand. I climb into the passenger seat of his car, and he hums under his breath all the way home, eyes on the road, while I stare out the window at white lane lines in the headlights. The house is dark when we get home. *I guess Mom didn't wait up.*

"Go to bed, baby girl," Dad says and kisses me on the top of the head, giving me a little shove in the direction of my room.

I do, without a word.

The house is silent when I get up the next morning. Well, not really morning, more like noon. I glance out the window and see my car already back in the driveway. *Dad must have been up and out early.* I head to the kitchen, hoping no one is around. On the counter, underneath my car keys, is a note from Mom saying I am grounded for taking off without telling anyone and for hiding in the baptismal. She is asking me to meet her at Cornerstone Counseling at two for an appointment with a counselor.

Who's the one who needs counseling here?

I grab a yogurt from the fridge and go outside to sit by the pool. The Sacramento sun does not kid around. As the blaze bounces around on the pool's surface like a kid on a trampoline, no clouds interfere. I sit on the edge, feet in tepid water, heat from the tile burning into the backs of my thighs, and spoon lemon yogurt onto my tongue. Photinia shrubs and pyracantha along the far side of the pool create a privacy screen and provide the only shade. This house came with a professionally landscaped front yard as dictated by the HOA, but the backyard is a shitshow. Mom, who does not exactly have a green thumb, threw whatever was on clearance at Home Depot into the planter bed. She didn't notice that pyracantha has thorns worthy of the crown of Jesus. I like plants, though. I planted a little sprig of lemon balm behind the shrubs.

I rinse my yogurt cup out at the spigot—that still doesn't have a hose—and fill it up. I step behind the planter toward my spindly lemon balm sprout and pour the yogurt cup of water around its base, wishing I could pinch off a few leaves to eat. It's still too weak to spare any foliage, so I kneel in the dirt—which is more leftover construction gravel than soil—my nose toward the struggling lemon balm, trying to get a whiff. Something moves under the red leaves of the photinia. I freeze as a rattlesnake slithers into the shadows.

My vision blurs and a shiver runs through me, as if a cloud has just covered the sun. Dust and a strange bitterness mix with chemically engineered lemon flavoring and rancid dairy in the back of my throat. As my vision clears, shadows of the glossy, green-and-garnet leaves dance beyond the ring of shade made by the shrub, their pointed tips waving in contradictory directions in the noontime glare. The surface of the pool is still and sharp as glass. Now that the snake has vanished, I long to slip over the cool speckled granite and stretch out into the shade.

Instead, two weeks later, I am sitting once again in the waiting room at Cornerstone Christian Counseling—having succumbed to Mom's initial appointment—focusing on the click and hum of the AC to tune out the hypnotizing hymns filtering through the office speakers.

Whoa-oh-ooohhhh, where there is faith . . . I believe in giving of myself for someone else . . .

Permanent butt-cheek hollows indent the pine-green upholstery of the reception armchairs, their curved wooden arms worn white wherever the varnish has rubbed off. In one corner, the grime is wedged so deeply into the fronds of plastic potted ferns it would take a firehose to clean it out. *Not that anyone will ever go to the trouble.*

I swivel around, and my elbow bumps a rickety, round table, knocking a smooth stone paperweight off a stack of business cards for *Cornerstone Christian Counseling* and *Bible-Based Life Coaching.* "Build your foundation on the Rock," the cards say. *God forbid they send me to an actual therapist.* I pick up the oval, black-and-white paperweight, rubbing its cool, silky surface back and forth against my palms, feeling the stone grow warm. Granite, I think. Next to the business cards is a stack of brand-new brochures from Church of the Third Angel with a picture of my parents on the front. I pick up the puke-pink flyer and roll the corner between my fingers, my throat closing as I read:

Recommit, Reconnect & Renew Couples' Retreat™
Hosted by Brother & Sister Leon Wolfe!
Reserve your spot for a weekend away with your spouse.
Hear how the Lord restored the Wolfes' marriage to better than ever!
Recommit, Reconnect & Renew your vows of holy matrimony.
Meals included. Renewal ceremonies extra.

Join us for Worship every Sunday!
Services at 8:00 a.m., 10:00 a.m., and 7:00 p.m.
Miracles Academy™ enrolling now!
Join Sister Delfa's team of Healers today!

I look at my exquisitely groomed mother's picture on the front of the brochure, the corner rolled into a tight curl, damp from my sweaty fingers. I fold and refold the paper into a triangle, unfold, refold. The counselor said that forgiveness was mine to give and receive. No one has asked me for forgiveness, and I don't think I have done anything wrong. The gist seems to be that I should apologize for hiding in the Purification Chamber instead of helping with the Fire Tunnel and not doing my part to help save souls. Like, someone's trip to Hell could be all my fault because I wasn't there to pray with them. And I have to forgive my mother for basically being a pedophile. Mom swears nothing happened and I apparently misunderstood the whole thing. Tony was just having some problems and wanted advice and prayer. But I know what I saw, and no matter how hard I try, I can't pretend I don't. I tried talking to Tony about it, but he literally blocked me. I haven't seen him since. Someone said he went to live with his dad.

The office door creaks open and the counselor pokes his comb-overed head into the waiting room.

"Rae Ann? Your turn," he says with a pasted-on smile full of long, yellow teeth.

As I follow the counselor into his office, the sound of the air conditioner turns into the crash of a waterfall inside my head.

three

Rebecca

"Tony and I just got a little too close," I explain to Leon the morning after the baptismal debacle. We're in the Hummer on our way to retrieve Rae Ann's car. "Tony's been struggling with alcohol pressures from his football team—you know how those boys are. They're just wild. He's trying to resist temptation, and we got to talking while he was doing chores for me at the church. Tony is a sweet kid, but he needs some guidance. You know, boys need a strong hand and his dad isn't around. Sister Delfa just babies him. He needs someone to talk to, and I thought I could help. You're right, though, I never should have gone up there alone with him—I didn't realize how he felt about me, but I should have seen it coming." I can feel myself starting to babble. I take a deep breath and focus on calming my shakes before continuing. "I was so surprised when he hugged me. I'm so naïve sometimes. Fortunately, we were able to pray through it. Thank you for stepping up to baptize him. I know it meant a lot to Sister Delfa and I think Tony really feels filled with the Spirit now. I'm sure he'll get over his little crush."

I eye Leon, wondering if he believes me.

"I hope so, Rebecca," he finally answers. "You forget how good-looking you are. Boys will be boys, and he lost control of himself. He got stars in his eyes looking at you. Rae Ann took it wrong and got overly upset. I'm worried she's distracted from her walk with the Lord by all this. We need to get her refocused. Thank God she had her phone turned on last night. I didn't want to call the police to help me find her. Although maybe I should have—put the fear of God in her a little bit. Heh, heh."

"Yeah, maybe," I snort and adjust in my seat, looking out the window again. "Good Lord. That girl is out of control to take off like that. I don't know what she was thinking. And to hide up in the Purification Chamber? That's just so selfish. She needs to be with us, helping us pray with people. I'm worried about her spiritual life too."

I put my hand on Leon's thigh, rubbing my thumb back and forth while he drives. "I'm worried she's going in the wrong direction. She needs some straightening out. Maybe we should send her to one of those reformation camps."

"Well, let's get her some help around here first," Leon suggests. "Set her up with Cornerstone Counseling. Let's not come down too hard on her just yet. She's confused. She'll come around."

"Okay, that's a good idea, baby." I nod, taking my hand away. *Sending Rae Ann off somewhere would look bad, anyway.* "Speaking of counseling . . . since we're on the subject, I've been meaning to talk to you about Sister Sarah. She is such a sweet soul, but I need to warn you, Leon, I sense her attraction to you. I know she's a plain little thing and not anywhere near pretty enough for you to notice, and likely lonely too. And, you're providing spiritual guidance, which—no doubt—she needs. But sometimes that can make a woman feel something they ought not, and I can tell she's feeling a pull toward you. I'm afraid you might find yourself in a situation like I did with Tony. Might get out of control. Do you know what I mean, baby?"

I doubt Leon knows about the camera. The IT guy swore Leon would never see it. *I'm giving Leon the chance to do the right thing here. It's only fair and it's not too late for us to get back on track.*

Tears well up in Leon's eyes. "I felt sorry for her, Rebecca. She took advantage of my sympathy."

I listen to him tiptoeing around his inappropriateness with Sister Sarah, although he stops short of a full confession. He talks, but I don't really listen, twisting my wedding rings around my finger.

Leon pulls the Hummer into the parking lot beside Rae Ann's hand-me-down Oldsmobile and cuts the motor. He turns and runs his thick finger along my jaw, gently grasping my chin and giving it his usual little shake. Then he reaches for me, his strong hands—my anchor since I was seventeen years old—pulling me to him.

"I'm sorry for my waywardness, Rebecca."

"I forgive you, Leon."

He prays out loud, holding my hands, and the Lord just descends into the car. I feel tears coming too. I pray also, silently though, and ask the Lord for forgiveness for not being vigilant. Leon pulls me into his lap and I bury my face in the folds of his scrubbed neck, breathing in his old-man aftershave, the smell of his skin underneath. Heavy arms hold me close, weighing me down.

We sit like that for a long time, breathing each other in. After a while, Leon climbs out of the Hummer, gasses up Rae Ann's Olds, and hops in to drive it home. *He loves driving that old tank.* I follow him in the Hummer, keeping him in sight as we barrel toward home in the early morning light.

The hour driving home gives me time to spin down new trails of thought. Leon is right. Cornerstone Counseling will do Rae Ann good. Get her sorted out. Hopefully, Tony knows better than to open his mouth. Still, I'll talk to Sister Delfa about his need for more discipline to be on the safe side. I feel so full of the Spirit and so happy to have this near-miss behind us. *The Lord just saved our marriage.* I believe that. Which brings me to the next thought: *How many other couples could use a reset? A little reconnection?* If Jesus can heal this rift for us, just think how our testimony can help other marriages. We could set up a couples' retreat . . . and charge a fortune for marriage counseling sessions, sharing circles, and wine tasting. And live music. Oh my Lord, we could set up an altar with fresh flowers and have vow renewal ceremonies. With styling services and a photographer. And custom cakes. *This is gold.*

My thoughts race as I drive without paying attention, cutting through Old Roseville on Main Street, remembering our little shoebox of a house in the old neighborhood. Before I know it, I am speeding down Baseline Road, headed west toward the Sacramento River. I don't realize where I am going until expansive fields open up on either side of the road, glowing gold in the sunrise.

Suddenly, I realize where I am headed. Delfa lives in a shacky little house out on East Levee Road overlooking the flood plains. As I stop to turn left on East Levee, a familiar red Ford Focus makes a right-hand turn onto Baseline without stopping at the sign. I check my rearview and see that red dot tearing east. What's Sarah doing out here?

As my Hummer rumbles over the levee, I roll my windows down, blackbirds rise and fall in the fields. Delfa's house is set back from the road, past the railyard, at the end of an unpaved, pothole-dented drive. *This must be a mess in the winter.* I pull up fast, breaking hard, spraying gravel. Delfa sits on her front porch swing like she is waiting for me. I hop down out of the Hummer and tiptoe over a muddy patch, sparing my white-soled Stella McCartney Adidas sneakers. Step up onto the wonky porch steps.

"Morning, Delfa."

Fingers stacked with silver rings, her knobby-knuckled hands grip a thick coffee mug. *Good Lord, does she sleep with all those rings on? That would drive me crazy.*

"Morning, Rebecca." Delfa takes a sip of coffee. The smell makes my mouth water.

Delfa's face is pale and tired-looking, yesterday's mascara smudged beneath her eyes. *I'm probably not looking too hot myself, but at least I washed my face and put on a bra.*

"Have a seat," she says, scootching over on the porch swing. "You want coffee or tea?"

"Coffee, thanks. With nonfat, no-sugar vanilla creamer if you don't mind."

Delfa heaves herself to her feet with a sigh and picks up a dirty cup from a round side table. *A dirty cup of half-drunk coffee with no ring around the inside, like someone just set it there. Fresh-dirty, not old-dirty.*

"Actually, I don't have any creamer at all. Sorry about that. I drink it black."

"Good grief, are you serious?" I laugh, shaking my head. "All right, well, just tea then." *Who doesn't keep creamer on hand?*

I sit on the swing, adjusting a flat flowered pillow under my rear. Looking out across the fields beyond the levee, not a cloud in the sky, just a vast expanse of bright blue from here to San Francisco. Delfa comes back out to the porch with a steaming mug of tea for me and a coffee refill for herself. I take a tentative sip. The bitter brew scalds the roof of my mouth and tea leaves catch on my tongue. *Good Lord, doesn't she use tea bags? What the hell is this? Foraged bark?* Delfa pulls a rumpled wax paper bag out of the pocket of her loose linen pants and plops it onto the table, which is in dire need of sanding and fresh paint.

"Made some brittle—pine nuts instead of peanuts this time, they were on sale—with some black pepper and ginger. You might like it."

Delfa's nut brittle is legendary around Miracles Academy. It's an old-fashioned kind of thing and the kids think it's weird, which it is. So many calories too. It's basically sugar, butter, and nuts—and hell on your teeth.

"Oh, no thanks, Delfa. It's a little early for candy for me!" I give her a big smile to show her I appreciate the gesture.

Delfa lowers herself onto the porch swing, which creaks under her rear, tucks her bare toe in the floorboard crack, and sets the swing in a slow, back-and-forth rhythm. Tea sloshes in my cup and I plant my Stellas on the floor to stop the sway of the swing. *That constant motion is going to make me seasick.*

"Was that Sarah I saw leaving? What was she doing out here?"

I snap off a corner of brittle and take a nibble despite myself. *Ugh. Damn it, that's good.*

Delfa pretends she can't hear me over the sound of the train going by and doesn't answer. The train lets out a long whistle so loud the tracks could be coming through the yard, which they practically are. *Why in the world does she live out here?*

Delfa sits there looking at me, her green eyes gone dark. I avert my gaze to the rice paddies in the distance and drop the subject of Sarah. Sip my tea, flecks of whatever floating in it lodged in my throat, black pepper on my tongue. All of a sudden, I feel scratches on my arms and look down. I am standing in the middle of a field of dry summer weeds practically up to my shoulders. Vultures circle above, pitch black against brilliant blue. Blackbirds rise and fall in dead golden grass, calling to each other in shrill nails-on-chalkboard screeches. My skin itches and my shoes are gone, field stubble piercing the soles of my feet, the smell of decay in my nose.

The swing creaks under Delfa and I am back on the porch. My tea is cold, floating bits sunk to the bottom of the cup. "I'm just going to use your restroom, if I may, Delfa," I murmur and step inside her front door, shaking.

What in hallucinatory fuck just happened?

Nothing like that has ever happened to me before. Is this Satan's work? I'm all shook up inside and looking around Delfa's tiny box of a living room doesn't help. The room is a cross between a natural history museum and a thrift shop. Ragged rugs and squat hand-me-down chairs. Piles of rocks and bones in front of tattered books line the shelves of an antique mahogany bookcase with glass doors. A carved key sticks out of the lock. I take a closer look, spotting a raven skull and what must be snake vertebrae sitting in the dust.

Jesus fucking Christ. I've visited before, but I've never been inside. Amethyst and quartz, a carved bone amulet on a leather cord. *That stuff might actually be worth something. Maybe she could sell it and fix this place up.* The top of the case is a jumble of old photographs in tarnished silver frames, faded sepia, anonymous faces looking back at me. Then I see something that makes the hair on the back of my neck stand up. A small square photograph tucked in the corner of a larger frame. An old couple: a fat woman in a green housedress and a little skinny man in suspenders, both dour. She is round as a house and he is about a third her size. I pluck out the picture and flip it over. On the back, it says "Ma and Pa Harlan, Pocatello, Idaho, 1910." I've seen this picture before. I know I have. I tuck it into my bag.

I go down the hall looking for the bathroom. I stand in front of the mirror staring at myself. *What the hell just happened out there? Am I losing my mind? Why does Delfa have a picture of my great-grandparents?* I take a breath and fix my lipstick. I use the facilities, trying to touch as few surfaces as possible, even though the bathroom— unlike the living room—is spotless. I take a deep breath and remind myself why I am here.

On the way back to the porch, I peek into Tony's bedroom. *He isn't there, thank goodness. Lord, what a mess.* I stick my head all the way into the room and take a deep breath, hoping for a whiff of him. All I smell is adolescent funk with undertones of unwashed socks. *Jesus.*

"Your living room looks like Rae Ann's bedroom, rocks and bones everywhere!" I say as I step out onto the porch. "Like nature just crawls right in through the windows!" I laugh out loud and settle back onto that flimsy excuse for a pillow.

Delfa just stares back with glimmering black eyes. *I could've sworn her eyes were green.*

"Listen, Delfa, let me tell you why I'm here. I am concerned about the rumors going around about Tony's football team and some inappropriate behavior. Drinking and that kind of thing. I know boys will be boys, but it's a bad example for the child of one of our team members to misbehave. Perhaps he needs a firmer hand, disciplinarily speaking, if you know what I mean."

Delfa creaks the swing, gazing out at the sky.

I clear my throat. "I think it would be best if Tony gets the help he needs, maybe from his dad down in San Diego? A boy his age needs a father around. Anyway, that type of thing reflects badly on the church. I mean, we're trying to save souls here, after all. We can't have that going on in our leadership. We would hate to have to let you go."

Delfa does not say a word. Not one word. Just looks out at the yard, past the gray branches of dead sycamore, staring into space. It gets weird after a minute, so I say, "Well, you think about it and let me know what you decide, Delfa. I'm sure Tony's dad would be happy to have him."

Still no answer.

"All righty then, I need to get going."

I stride back to my Hummer, swinging my Chloé bag over my shoulder. Climb into the driver's seat, slide on my classic Ray-Bans, turn the key, and give Delfa a wave, which she does not see as she is still staring off at nothing. I pull out onto East Levee toward Baseline and look back at her house, expecting to see her still on the porch. But somehow, she is now all the way back in the field behind the house. Standing out there in the weeds by the train tracks, looking away from me, toward the east. Holding out her arms like she can catch the wind, her cotton candy hair flying around all over the place. Storm clouds are piling up fast in that direction, silver and gray with a roiling black and purple center, like an immense, pulsing bruise. Rolling over the field like they're coming for me.

We were not supposed to have weather today, so I don't know where this storm is coming from. But as I turn onto Baseline, I see that I am headed straight into it.

Story Two:
Pocatello 1910

Rebecca

My spine collides with the rough pine of the pew, and a sharp burn spikes through my shoulder blades, vibrating down through my gut, as blood and pain radiate from my bitten tongue. Ma kept on dancing around and speaking in tongues, like she didn't even know the back of her hand smacked me off my feet. Maybe she didn't and maybe she did. When the Spirit moves and Ma gets rolling, her limbs fly around like they're trying to ward off a swarm of hornets. *My fault for getting too close.* I stay put on the pew, paying closer attention now, ducking when her wild arm swings my way. I rest my arms across my belly, feeling it churn and bloat. At least she hadn't walloped me there. Ma stops flailing in front of me, slows to swaying and garbling with her eyes closed. I hang my head and pretend to say a prayer, checking to see if my lower belly is pooching out yet. I always wear loose dresses anyway, so I can hide for a while longer, but it is for sure time to talk to Leon. He keeps coming around, even though his pa told him to keep clear of me, which Leon let slip. Apparently, me and Delfa have a reputation. For what, I wonder. I was mostly a virgin when I met Leon and Delfa is still a kid.

Anyway, church is winding down, thank the Lord. The preacher is droning one last come-to-Jesus hymn and my gaze drifts out the open window. Anyone coming to Jesus had come to him at this point. Blinding noontime sun bakes dry-as-a-bone fields that stretch toward town, and heat pulses into the dim shadow of the sanctuary, intensifying the smell of sweat and pine. As the congregation gathers themselves to exit, I cast a look over my shoulder, spotting Brother Jim lurking at the back. You couldn't miss all six-foot-five of that guy if you tried. Those long arms could get a hand up a skirt without anyone seeing his body move, as every girl in the First Pentecostal Church of Pocatello knows. I wait on that pew till he goes out first, although since I turned fourteen, Brother Jim mostly leaves me alone. I hold onto Delfa's arm to keep her with me because she's still only twelve.

Back at the house, I settle onto the rickety porch chair to wait for Leon. Bannock Range slopes blue against the horizon, rivulets of snow still cradled in winding crevices despite the heat. A swath of deep-green trees brushes the base of the mountains. From across the fields, tumbleweed and sage float on the air with the musty stench of sheep shit and wool. I can see the rooftops of town, only just. Schoolhouse, railroad station, Center Street where the bank, shops, and saloons huddle together against the wind. The railyard is not visible from there as it is down on the Portneuf River, but once in a while, a team of horses rumbles by, headed in that direction. The logs they pull will see more of Idaho than anyone on this porch as the Portneuf empties into the Snake River and out of here. Horses and wagons rattle and creak past the house to the railroad station too, piled high with wooden crates of peas, apricots, apples, pears, and burlap bags of potatoes smelling of earth, lurching ahead of dust billows from the dirt roads. On occasion, a crate bounces loose and me and Delfa grab buckets to scoop up the scattered produce. We aren't too good to glean.

I shift the porch chair back and forth, squeaking the legs, impatient. The sound annoys Hank, Pop's perpetually sleeping mongrel. Hank twitches, and the fly on his back lifts and settles again onto his bristled white fur. The only other house within shouting distance is another ramshackle, clapboard cabin just like this one, parked in the middle of a dirt patch. Like this one. Laundry flapping in wind. Not snow-white knickers dancing on a breeze against blue sky. No. Raggedy long-johns incapable of fully relinquishing their grime, anchored to a dragging clothesline with quadruple clothespins, are punished by the incessant wind of the Idaho plains, as are we all.

I keep my eyes on the road toward town, watching, trying not to hear—but I can't not hear—Ma and Pops arguing from inside the kitchen. Ma slamming the skillet onto the stovetop more forcefully than anybody needs to like she always does when she's mad. The slap of water on bare earth from the wash pan, the empty pan clattering onto the hook by the door. Ma can cook, clean, and fight at the same time. Pops is probably hunkered down in his chair, waiting for her storm to blow over. He's not one to fight back much.

Ma. Honey Venus Harlan. Rumors of her past followed me around at the high school, which is why I quit going. Kids whispered that she got here by following the railroad crews. Where the crews go, whatever they might spend their money on will follow, and that includes women. I don't believe it, though, because Ma is as big around as she is tall, and I can't picture anybody paying for that. Ma says her family comes from Mississippi and she still carries a slow Southern drawl. She won't say why she left, only that her family had money and she left it all behind. Pops came out working on the railroad and somehow he and Ma got stuck with each other. Then Ma found religion and Pops found the saloon.

Everybody here in Pocatello is from somewhere else, except for the Shoshone. Most folks intended to end up farther down the road, like California. The Mormons came, running from vigilante justice in Missouri. Prospectors came looking for gold and silver, then along came the Overland Stagecoach Trail, followed by the railroad. And now, it's a town. Pocatello turned into a pocket of people stranded halfway to elsewhere. The Shoshone got shoved farther and farther away from the river and into the hills. Once in a while, stragglers desperate for food wander around the outskirts of town or into the saloons looking for work or a drink.

Leon's homemade wagon rattles into the yard in a cloud of white dust. I land on the hot leather bench seat next to him before the screen door finishes banging shut behind me, press up against his lean thigh, hands to myself, like he always tells me. The tang of sweat from underneath his cotton shirt fills my nose. I clench my fingers together.

"Rebecca, I was coming up to get you. At least let me help you up," Leon says.

"Nope, no need. Let's go." I bounce on the seat.

We rumble down the gravel road to the river just past town. Leon pulls onto the ledge above the riverbank and slows the horse to an easy stop.

"Never trust the horse," Leon says with a smile.

"Aren't we going to your tent?" I ask, stroking his thigh.

Leon lives in a little pitched tent while building a house and working shifts at the railyard. He can build anything. He is only seventeen and his hands are already hard. He left home at fourteen to escape his pa's fist. If he can get the house done by end of summer, he'll have squatter's rights and the government can't take it away when the town boundaries are set in the fall; at least that's what they're saying at the railyard. I make Leon tell me everything they say at the railyard. I like to know what's going on.

Now that Pocatello is here to stay, the town is building up fast. The same guy that built the railroad—some rich old man named Murray—supplies whatever the citizens need and then charges them for it. Like water pipes. The Portneuf has enough water for ten towns, but traipsing down to the river with a bucket is no way to live, so old Murray built water pipes to downtown and the west side. Some folks have water coming all the way into their house, I heard. Just turn the handle and water comes out. I would like to see that. Most of us still have pumps in the yard and outhouses though, which is better than hauling buckets like the boxcar people do. The water pipes don't extend out to Leon's place yet, but maybe someday.

Leon clears his throat and lifts my hand away from his thigh. I clutch his thick fingers, rubbing my thumb over the dry bump of his calloused palm. Leon grabs my hand and holds my fingers tight.

"Listen, Rebecca. I have something to say to you."

I lean in and kiss his chin. *If he thinks he's leaving me, he's wrong.*

"What is it?" I whisper, my lips right up close to his mouth.

"I've been praying on marriage all week. The Lord has called me to preach and I can't do that if we're sinning. Let's get married, Rebecca. It's the right thing."

"Yeah, of course, Leon." I kiss his chin again, right on the dimple. "Might as well. We're gonna have a baby anyhow," I say with a grin.

He sits silently, squinting at the water rushing past, the wild chop catching sunlight and throwing it downriver, shadow and light leapfrogging toward the Snake.

"Well, it's the Lord's will, then," Leon says somberly.

Not exactly a sonnet, but it'll do, I think. "We best not waste time, Leon. I missed two cycles already. How about next Sunday after church? Everybody will already be there and we can do vows real quick and go back to the house for lunch. No need to put it off, your folks won't come anyway. And, it'll be my fifteenth birthday!"

"That'll do." Leon looks into my eyes and smiles. His eyes crinkle at the corners when the smile hits them. He reaches for my hand and kisses it.

"Praise God," he breathes.

I turn my head away so he can't see me roll my eyes. I am not sure the Lord has anything to do with this. But, no more flying skillets, no more shrieking Ma. A little house. A little baby. Delfa will have to figure out her own escape.

"Come on, now. Let's go back to the tent," I whisper.

"No, Rebecca. We are going to wait until after the wedding like we should have in the first place," Leon says in his stern voice.

I giggle. I can't help it.

"I'm already pregnant, Leon. What harm can it do?"

"It's not right in the eyes of God. Also, I am going to spend the afternoon working on our house. Let me take you home and talk to your pa. Then, I'll get to work."

The next Sunday, after the quickest vows you've ever heard, me and Leon go back to the house for cake with Ma, Pops, and Delfa. I wear a white lace dress and veil borrowed from the neighbor and Pops takes our picture. It is my fifteenth birthday and

Delta is not speaking to me. Ma gives me a pat on the arm as she hands me her old leather satchel.

"Here's your clothes, Rebecca. I'm gonna need that satchel back when you can. Y'all have a good day, now," she says, practically herding us out the door.

"Okay, thank you, Ma," I say while Leon and Pops shake hands like they made a deal. "Bye, Delta. Come see me tomorrow. I'll meet you in town."

Delta crosses her arms, glares at me, and turns away. I come from a long line of hard-hearted women.

I let Leon help me into the wagon since everyone is watching and we drive to the house. Leon has put up half the roof since last Sunday, but we don't have a door or windows yet, so he pitched the tent on the dirt floor inside. I pull back the canvas tent flap and crawl in. Cotton blankets are folded up in a tidy pile in the middle of the tent with two pillows stacked on top and one slightly wilted white daisy, just for me.

"Welcome home, my dear," Leon says with a grin as he climbs in behind me.

"Come here," I laugh and pull him onto the stack of blankets.

The next morning, Leon leaves before dawn to work a shift at the railyard. I stretch out between the blankets, alone in bed for the first time ever in my life. I have always shared a bed with Delta. I turn onto my side and curl around my stomach to take the pressure off my bladder, and drift back into sleep, dreaming of a churning in my belly. In my dream I can see right through my skin to two babies rolling around inside me. They don't look like babies though; they look like little naked men and one is hairy all over. The other one is small and smooth and swims around the hairy one like an eel. They punch and grab and kick each other and I wake up, vomit rising in my throat. I open the tent flap and find the slop bucket in the corner. Just enough daylight leaking into the house for me to see what I am doing. *It sure would be nice to have water pipes right into the house*, I think as I take a sip of water from the bucket Leon filled for me before he left for work. I rinse out my mouth and spit bile into the slop pail.

The fresh air of early morning calms my stomach and I shake off the memory of my strange dream. Distant rumblings come from the railyard and someone's roosters are up and at it. I stand in the open doorway of our little shell of a house and breathe it in, rub my belly, and feel the baby flutter under my hand.

I have some things to figure out, like who is going to help me have this baby since I know we can't pay for the hospital. And how I am going to cook with no kitchen. And how to convince Leon that there isn't any money in preaching. But right now in this moment, the stars are fading as Bannock Range glows pink and I am alone in the silence.

five

About Delfa

Late summer came and my belly is really poking out now. Fall, snow, and this baby are all right around the corner. Me and Leon are settled in, him at the railyard and me figuring out how to be. I am so antsy I can't be still; months of being trapped in our one-room house loom. Yesterday after work, Leon said the rumor around the railyard was that Delfa had been hanging around down at the saloon all gussied up with lipstick and maybe I should do something about that, seeing as how she is now only thirteen and a little young for a reputation. *Do what about it?* I wonder. She's just following in Ma's footsteps. I figure things are rough for her at Ma and Pop's with me gone, but I don't know what I'm supposed to do about that.

So, I say to Leon, "Let's get her out of here for a few days. We could go to see your family. I still haven't met 'em." Thinking to myself, *I can show them I'm not anyone to be ashamed of.*

"I only have Sundays off work," Leon reminds me. "And there's church."

"We can skip church for once, can't we? You aren't the preacher yet."

"It won't look good for the assistant pastor to skip a service, Rebecca."

"It's just once. Why are you so perturbed about it? Just say we need to visit your ma. We could stop at Bear River on the way and pick huckleberries. The church isn't gonna fall apart if you miss one Sunday."

By this point, Leon has fled to the outhouse and I am talking to the back door. We're going, though. I can't wait to get out of this house for a day. I spend the afternoon packing up and trying to get a message to Delfa to be ready early Sunday morning. Maybe I should leave a note at the saloon.

Next Sunday morning, we rattle into Ma's yard and Delfa is waiting on the porch like I used to wait for Leon. She barrels out the screen door and launches herself onto the seat beside me. Everybody is always ready for a rescue from that house. We take off, heading south toward Bear River, bouncing around on the rutted road, hot breeze whipping my hair into Leon's face until he yells at me to tame it. I laugh and shake my head like a wild woman. It's good to get out.

We watch for the turnoff to Bear River. It isn't really a road, just an old Shoshone trail. I know I will remember it because Pops brought me and Delfa here to fish. There are fishing spots closer to home, but Pops likes to get out of the house too. Delfa was little so she doesn't remember it much.

"Slow down, Leon, it's coming up soon," I yell at him, because this bend in the road is just right and I can hear the water running.

Leon slows the horse and leans forward, studying the side of the road like the turn is going to jump out at him.

"There it is," I about scream, so excited to get out of this rickety wagon. "Delfa, do you remember?"

"Maybe," she whispers.

Leon pulls onto the path and tree branches poke his and Delfa's faces. I'm in the middle, so the branches don't reach me. All of a sudden, the riverbank opens up and a blue-green stretch of river slides by. The wagon lurches to a stop and we pile out, me and Delfa holding hands and running for the water, stumbling over roots and rocks, me holding my belly with one hand. Me and Delfa rip off our boots, hike up our skirts, and wade right in while Leon ties up the horse. We all take turns in the bushes and then I spot a side trail that winds up into the scrubby trees.

"Let's go look for huckleberries!" I holler.

"You girls go. I'm going to take a nap," Leon says.

Delfa grabs the bucket and Leon stretches out on a blanket, pulling his hat down over his eyes. Me and Delfa traipse up the trail, swatting flies, the cicadas buzzing loud in the shrubs, little whipsnakes slithering out of our way, fast as lightning.

"Remember, this is where the huckleberries were that time we came with Pops."

"Is it?" Delfa is vague.

"Yeah, come on. I can't believe you don't remember."

"I was only three, I think."

"Yep! Here they are!"

We come upon the huckleberry bushes, loaded with ripe berries. *We better watch out for bears*, I think, but I don't say it out loud or Delfa will want to go back. We gobble berries, a sparse few going into the bucket at first. It's not often you get something as sweet as that. Our dresses get hung up on the bushes and our fingers run purple, but we don't care. We fill up on berries and then start picking in earnest. If we can get a bucketful, we can take some to Leon's ma. I doubt we can pick enough to last us all the way home, as hungry as I am all the time.

The huckleberry path curves back down toward the river and wild onions and mushrooms sprout by the trail as the earth gets damp. We pick a few to nibble, but after the berries, they don't taste so good. The sharp smell of ripe berries in the hot glow of late summer shifts into a wetter, denser scent of rotten logs and algae as we approach the water's edge. It's been a dry summer and the river is low and dank at the shore.

"Let's walk along the water back to Leon," I suggest, thinking the route will be quicker.

"Mmmm . . ." Delfa mumbles. She has hardly said a word all day.

We pick our way over the river rocks, stopping to look upstream to the dust-colored stone valley walls hovering above the quiet flow of the water. It's strange how you can tell the water is moving, but it looks perfectly still at the same time. Like the surface isn't going anywhere but it's moving underneath. From a distance, the river looks blue and serene, and then up close, you can see it churn. The water is greenish-black where the shrubs meet the shore and we have to wade in to get around the overgrowth. I hold a prickly branch back to let Delfa stoop under and, as she is navigating under the branch and around my belly, she lets out a gasp.

"What are you doing? Hurry up!" I yell.

Delfa is always finding things, but now is not the time. I am holding the branch in between thorns and it's catching in my hair. Delfa pops up on the other side of me.

"Look at this," she says, holding up a braided leather strap, skinny as a shoelace, with a little piece of carved bone or something attached. "This was wrapped around the underside of that bush."

Delfa holds the strap out to me and I run my fingers over it. Stiff and brittle, like it's been there for a long, long time, the carving worn away to mystery. It causes me to shiver and I hand it back to her.

Delfa holds that strap and rubs the amulet on her cheek, sniffing it.

"What in the world are you doing, Delfa?" I ask as she runs her tongue along the edge, rubbing her hands on it like it's a pet cat. She doesn't answer me, of course.

The rocks are slimy and our feet sink into the mud and little squiggly, swimming things nibble our toes while she pets this piece of old leather and bone.

I shake my toes off. "Come on, Delfa, let's keep going."

Delfa doesn't answer but stands stock-still staring up the valley, wrapping that leather cord around her hand till her knuckles turn white. The bone amulet hangs down, catching the light.

I grab her arm. "Come on."

"Wait," she whispers.

Delfa is breathing fast and shallow like she can't catch air.

"Wait for what?"

"Do you see her?"

"What? See who?"

"I see her. I see . . ." Delfa murmurs, whimpering like she has stomach pain.

"What do you see? Delfa, are you sick? What is it?"

Delfa starts to shake and tremble like something got ahold of her. She is white as a sheet.

"Oh Lord, Delfa, are those berries coming up? Let me hold your hair if you're gonna throw up," I offer.

"No. No. Don't you see her? She is getting in the water. She's getting in the water with a baby on her back. She's wading in."

I'm looking where Delfa is looking, but I don't see anything. "Delfa, you're scaring me. What is wrong with you? There's nobody there."

But Delfa's eyes are all glassy and wild, so I shut up and strain my eyes toward the water, trying to see what she sees.

"She's all the way in. Someone is chasing her. They're coming, they're coming! She's up to her neck now, the baby is underwater." Delfa is wading into the river up to her knees. "She went under! We have to help her. She's swimming now, she's coming our way. Over here, over here!" Delfa screams out to no one.

I am truly afraid now. Delfa isn't right. There is no woman or baby or anyone chasing anything. And believe me, I am looking around like crazy for the evidence.

"No! NO!" Delfa screams. "They're shooting at the water. Where is she?"

Delfa's little body is racked with sobs now and a wild animal shriek gurgles out of her throat. She wades further into the water, flailing around, splashing right and left like she's looking for something that sunk, still gripping onto that leather strap.

"You come with me now, right now." I step into the water, grab Delfa's arm, and pull. I yank her as hard as I can and we stagger back onto the bank.

"NO! We can't leave her," Delfa cries. "She's gone, she's gone."

"Delfa, now! Come with me right now!" I holler and drag her along. We stumble together through the water's edge back to Leon, who is just rousing from his nap.

"Hey, what was that yelling about? You see a bear?" He sits up, sliding his hat back.

I shake my head at him and practically throw the bucket of berries into his lap. "Here ya go," I say, and wobbly-legged, I plop down beside him. "Delfa saw something, but I didn't." I don't want to explain what just happened. *Maybe it was a bear.*

Delfa sits on the blanket staring at the water, wrapping that leather strap around and around her knuckles, rubbing the worn-out piece of bone between her fingers.

"What's wrong with her?"

"Too many berries. I think maybe her stomach hurts," I say with a shrug.

Delfa hugs her knees in, rocking back and forth, and we leave her be.

What I am thinking but not saying is that I thought I saw a little Indian boy standing in the water, sucking his fingers and watching the same spot in the water where Delfa was staring. His glossy black hair hanging over round, baby cheeks, his little hands holding onto a clay pot. He was so real I could smell the buckwheat gravy in his bowl. That's all I need is to go crazy too, so I keep that thought to myself.

After a while, Delfa lies down, curls up around herself, and drifts off to sleep, and Leon starts kissing my hand. I know where this goes and it's fine with me. Now that we're married, such things put him in a good mood because he's free of guilt. I reach my hand around the back of his neck and kiss along his jawline.

"Hey, Leon," I say, looking up. "I hear the city is going to buy the water systems from that Mr. Murray fellow, pipes and all, the whole shebang. He about poisoned the whole town a few years ago, did you know about that? He never cleaned the filter screens and they were full of dead animals. Bunch of people got typhoid fever." I start a conversation while he is feeling happy.

"What in the world are you talking about, Rebecca? What's your sudden interest in Pocatello's water system?" Leon asks with a smirk. "Ohhhh, lemme guess . . . the city is hiring?"

"Well, it's not a bad idea, Leon. Pocatello is growing like crazy and a city job isn't a bad thing." I rub his leg. "Railyard work is hard on a body. You aren't gonna be young forever."

"And you want a house on the west side."

"Don't you? I know we aren't living in a boxcar like some, but it would be nice to have a floor and water pipes that run all the time. And I want to birth this baby in the hospital like a lady. Is that too much to ask?"

"You know the Lord has called me to preach, Rebecca. The railyard isn't forever. Besides, old Murray isn't going to give up rights to the water system that he built without a fight."

"'The Lord, the Lord, the Lord.' How well does the Lord pay?" I laugh and throw a huckleberry at his head right where his hairline is receding toward his ears. "We can't live on huckleberries and mushrooms. You're smart, Leon. Smarter than any of those other guys down at the railyard. You could just go work for Mr. Murray until the city buys the system and then they'll need you because you'll know how it all operates. Anyway, you can still preach on Sundays."

"I guess you have it all figured out." Leon sighs.

"As a matter of fact, I do." I laugh again. "You're welcome."

"All right, all right, I'll look into it." Leon kisses my cheek and rubs my belly. "We best get a move on if we're going to be at my folks' before dark."

Rebecca

The sun is just on its way down when me and Leon and Delfa pull up to Leon's parents' shack in the boonies and pile out of the wagon, our shadows long in the yard. No one comes running to greet us. No kids or dogs. I know Leon has younger siblings and it seems strange that they aren't outside on a nice evening. "Where's everybody at?" I ask him.

"Probably out back, I guess," Leon says, not seeming too eager to find them. "Helloooo!" he calls.

His greeting echoes into the encroaching twilight. *No answer.* We stand in the yard, unsure of what to do in the reverberating silence.

Leon steps up to the front door and pushes it open, pokes his head in and calls out, "Ma? Charlie?"

"Charlie is the next oldest," I tell Delfa, who is trailing behind me. "Probably about my age, actually."

Leon lets the door fall closed, looks at me, and shrugs. I can tell he's worried. At least four younger kids were here last time Leon checked. It makes no sense that the house would be left abandoned.

"Maybe they're in the barn," Leon says. "If the horse and cart are gone, I guess they will have gone somewhere. No idea how they would get everybody in that cart, though, or where they would go."

Leon walks quickly now around the side of the house toward the barn, and Delfa and I follow. He lifts the wire loop off the post and lets the gate to the chicken yard fall open. We step over and set it back up. I do not want to be blamed for losing their chickens before we even meet face to face. Leon stops just inside the barn door and I notice something strange about his stance. I step up beside him, peeking around his elbow.

"Ma?" Leon whispers, and then I see her.

"Charlie? Are you in here?" Leon calls, his voice breaking.

I feel Delfa gripping my waist and I do not know where to look. Shadows move, and Charlie steps out from behind a horse stall, followed by three younger kids. They look like they have seen the end of times, the little ones wide-eyed and silent.

"Leon?" Charlie whispers.

"Where's Pa?" Leon asks.

"Out in the fields. He'll be home soon, I guess," Charlie says with a shrug, his eyes turned away from his ma's body. I see his knees shaking.

"What happened?" Leon asks, even though it seems obvious.

"We found her like this," he says. "She's dead, isn't she?"

"I reckon so," Leon says. "Come on, come outta here."

He holds his arms out to the little ones and they step toward him, hanging onto Charlie like they're walking on a cliff edge.

"Hey Charlie, I'm Rebecca." I walk real slow over to him and inch my way in between the kids and their ma's body, her lifeless hand still clutching the gun. "Look here, you come in the house with me. We brought a bucketful of huckleberries and I sure could use a drink of water." I step a little closer, talking real soft, and one of the little ones rushes around Charlie's shaking legs and buries her face up against my balloon belly.

I pat her head. "Come on, then. Let's go inside."

"Charlie, I need you to stay with me," Leon says. "Please."

Delfa, thankfully paying attention for once, steps up behind me, takes the hand of the littlest one, and helps me herd them all out the barn door, all except Charlie. We clamber through the gate and into the little house through the back door. Not one of them says a word. We enter the dim light of the kitchen, such as it is.

"Delfa, could you please go get the huckleberries?" I ask, still moving slow. I am trying to stay calm, because I do not know what else to do.

Delfa looks at me with the eyes of a cornered rabbit and nods. The little one won't let go of her, so Delfa swings her up on one hip.

"Okay, now, where is that water pail?" I ask, moving from one thought to the next like I have never had a thought before, like my brain is trying to feel its way through the dark.

One of the middle kids points silently. I see the pail and lift its cover, pretending not to see the flies floating on the surface. I scoop the ladle and take a brackish sip. If we go out to the well for fresh water, we will see the barn. I need to keep these kids inside. I turn back toward them, panic sweat forming on my neck, big, round, empty eyes staring at me all around.

"When do you expect your pa to get home?" I ask the kids, just as I hear him stomp up the back step and bang into the house. *Oh, thank God.* The little ones run to his legs like moths to flame, and Leon's pa stops short and looks at me in surprise.

"Who might you be? Where's Sarah at?" he asks.

"I'm Rebecca. Ahhhh . . . Sarah's in the barn with Leon and Charlie, sir," I stammer. "But, ummm. Wait, please."

The little ones cling to his pant legs and I see the light dawn in his eyes that all isn't right. He peels the children off his legs and bursts back out through the door toward the barn. Then, I hear his howl. I look at Delfa coming in the door with the huckleberry bucket and she looks at me, turning vacant like she gets. I can see she isn't going to be helpful for much longer.

"All righty, kids, let's have some of these huckleberries. You like 'em, don't you?" I ask the kid nearest to me, who has transferred attachment to my skirt. I get a silent nod. *I'll take it.* I usher them into the main room of the house and see that is all there is to it—one bed and a couple of cots line the far wall, a fireplace to the right. Two chairs, a bench, and a rickety table. And I thought I was brought up poor. Delfa sets the bucket on the table and the kids crowd around, momentarily distracted by huckleberries.

Leon pokes his head in and his face looks old all of a sudden. "Rebecca, I'm going to need your help. You too, Delfa. Kids, you stay in the house, you hear me? We'll come back for you."

"Okay," I say and follow him out, Delfa behind me.

"Stay here. I mean it," Leon says to the kids.

"I wrapped Ma up in a horse blanket," Leon says to me once we're out of earshot. "But we can't put her in the ground like that. I put her in the wagon to take her down to the creek, but I need you two to wash her and get her ready for burial. It's not for me to do or Pa, either."

"What in the world, Leon? You want me to what? I have never washed a dead body before," I protest. "I haven't ever even *seen* one." This is beyond me.

"You've got to, Rebecca. I'm not asking you. I'm telling you. Do not fight me on this, not right now," Leon says in a voice I have never heard before. "I'll be helping Pa and Charlie dig her a grave in the pasture."

"All right, okay," I agree. "Okay, Delfa?"

Delfa nods silently, her gaze distant. Leon's pa brings out a cotton sheet with Sarah's other dress inside and hands it over. We pile in the wagon, Sarah's body a bundle in the back, and drive in silence through the pasture to the creek, last light bouncing off the bumpy ground. Leon pulls the bundle out of the back, carries his ma to the shallow creek, and lays her gently beside the water.

"I'll be back in a bit for you," Leon says and goes back to the wagon before I can yell at him to stay.

He can't do it. I can see that. Me and Delfa unwrap the densely woven, red-and-black horse blanket from Sarah's body just as the stars are coming out. She looks so young, lying on the blanket with her hair spread out and her face soft, the geometric pattern in the weave like jagged teeth. My fingers jitter and freeze as I unhook her dress and pull it from her upper body, threads sticking in the wound in her chest, coagulated blood fusing fabric to skin. I look at Delfa's face, but she is in shadow. She helps me peel the dress all the way off. Sarah wears nothing underneath. I guess there is no need for undergarments in the backwoods. No shoes, either.

We tear strips of her skirt, dip them in the creek, then squat beside her body to wash her face and hands, unsure of where to start. Delfa brushes Sarah's hair with her fingers, picking out hay from the barn floor. I grab another strip of skirt, hold it by the end, and let the creek water flow through until it's good and wet. I scoop as much water with it as I can to try to clean her wound. I think that's what I am supposed to do, but I just don't know how to do it. We will be here all night, dabbing away at the gaping hollow, and I don't know when Leon is coming back. There is no way to fix her.

"Hey, Delfa. Let's carry her into the water to get her clean," I say. "Lord knows she hasn't had a bath in a long while. Maybe it'll wash her sins away."

Delfa nods silently and we use the horse blanket to scooch Sarah down into the creek's flow. Cold black water ripples over the blanket's edge and around her, the obstruction of her body causing bubbles that catch the emerging moonlight and wash downstream. The creek is just deep enough to wade up to our ankles, and we scoop water in our palms and direct the flow up and over Sarah's calloused, dirty feet, up her legs, and into her privates. I have never seen a woman's body before, never even looked that closely at my own, so I am glad for the shadows. It seems brash to scrub her, so I open her legs a little to let the creek do the washing. Delfa rubs Sarah's scalp with her fingers and rinses her thin hair, which is just turning gray at the temples. Then, avoiding the wound, Delfa rubs grime from the soft pelt of Sarah's armpits while I scoop water onto Sarah's belly, immersed in the task.

"Hey, Delfa," I whisper. "Look here."

I run my hand over Sarah's lower belly, just below her navel. The moonlight is bright enough now to see a firm mound underneath the brown stripe that extends from her belly button down to her nethers, silver marks in her skin stretching over what could only be the beginnings of another baby. Delfa crawls around Sarah's body and places her hands on Sarah's belly, closes her eyes, and whispers something to herself, rocking back and forth on her knees in the creek as a full moon rises above us all. Delfa raises her face to the night sky. Her whispers flow into a singsong kind of chant, but I can't make out the words.

"Ready now, Delfa?" I whisper, afraid to break her spell but anxious to wrap Sarah up. My feet are soaked and freezing and I can't look at her anymore. Also, I think Delfa might have lost her mind, and I can't be out here with a crazy person and a dead body.

Delfa startles as if she's forgetting where she is, which she probably is. At least she is present enough to help me pull the soaking-wet horse blanket back up onto the bank. With no way to dry Sarah off, we struggle to get her Sunday dress onto her wet body as best we can, creek water and blood flowing from her chest. I am unable to do up the buttons at all, so we leave it loosely on her body, spreading the sheet out on the bank. Then, knowing there isn't any pretty way to do this, we roll Sarah over and onto the sheet and begin to wrap her up. But just before we close up the sheet, Delfa pulls the leather strap from the river out of her pocket and wraps it around Sarah's wrist, bends Sarah's elbows to cross her hands over her belly, and tucks that little bone amulet underneath her hands. We pull the sheet over Sarah's face.

Me and Delfa sit with Sarah under a full moon so bright the air pulses, until Leon's wagon rumbles onto the creek bank. The three of us lift her as gently as we are able into the back of the wagon. As I grab my skirt to climb in, Leon, who hasn't said a word, grips the back of my neck with his thick, trembling hand and pulls me close.

"Thank you, Rebecca," he murmurs into my ear and kisses my hair. I rub my cheek on his chest and hear his thudding heart. Squeeze his side with my frigid hand.

We haul back toward the house. Leon's pa and Charlie are digging a grave in the pasture. "Lord, Leon, why don't they wait until morning?"

"Flies. Wolves. Rats. Vultures. Coyotes. Bears."

"Oh."

We pull up to the gravesite and see the young ones curled up in the grass by the open pit. Me and Delfa go sit with them in silence and moonlight and they make their way into our laps and sleep, except for the littlest one, who is wide awake and watching. When the grave is ready, Pa, Leon, and Charlie lay Sarah to rest. Leon speaks a few words of prayer that do not register to my ears. They fill the grave with soil again and Pa and Charlie stack stones on top of the fresh earth to weigh it down and prevent digging critters. We pile the children into the wagon and the rest of us clamber in. Back at the house, we carry the little ones to their cots, all of us dreary with fatigue.

"I've got to be at the railyard at dawn, Pa. We best be going," Leon says with a sigh.

Delfa is already asleep when I climb into the wagon. Charlie rushes up to Leon's side.

"Let me come with you. Please, Leon, don't leave me here," Charlie stammers.

I see Leon hesitate, but his pa speaks first. "No, Charlie. You're to stay here. I need your help."

Charlie stares at Leon, his eyes screaming for rescue.

"I can get him on at the railyard, Pa. He's old enough," Leon offers, rubbing his tired face with his hand. "The church will help with the kids, won't they?"

"I said no. Get in the house, Charlie."

Leon sighs and flicks the reins. "All right. Sorry, Charlie."

He gives Charlie a look I can't quite make out, and the horse starts to pull out of the yard, real slow. I'm looking back at Pa and Charlie standing in the moonlit yard and, all of a sudden, Charlie breaks into a run and launches himself into the wagon bed. As soon as he does, Leon slaps the horse's flank with a shout and we barrel out onto the road. We speed through the night toward

Pocatello, Charlie hunkered down behind us, his pa's rage lost to the wind.

By the time next spring rolls around, Charlie is working in the railyard like the young man he is, Leon is the superintendent for the Pocatello Water Company, and baby Rae Ann is bouncing in my lap in the front room of our new house on the west side.

I walk down to meet Delfa at the shops, hoping she shows up this time, and hear a ruckus. *What now?* I wonder. We'd seen a fair amount of unrest throughout the winter because Leon's boss, Mr. Murray, hadn't buried the water pipes deep enough. They all froze, but he kept charging top dollar for ice. It was mighty inconvenient for all concerned, and the city council was trying to strong-arm Mr. Murray into selling them the water system.

A group is forming on Center Street and from what I can hear, it sounds serious. I wander over and see what's what.

When I get there, "what is what" is that this mob has my husband by the arms and everyone is waving guns around in his face. *Lord have mercy. None of this is Leon's fault!* I go running over, pram bouncing around on the cobblestones, and Rae Ann starts to howl.

"LEON," I scream out. "LET HIM GO! LET HIM GO!"

My heart is pounding out of my chest. Nobody looks my way or lets Leon go. All the men in town seem to have showed up to make a point. More and more people are gathering, most with guns and all of them yelling about the water situation. I push my way in, using Rae Ann's pram to bark a few shins.

"Let him go! LET HIM GO!" I am shrieking now, shoving through the crowd toward Leon. I can see from the look on his face, he thinks his time has come.

Just then, the sheriff comes running toward us, barking at everybody to settle down and go home. Says that old Mr. Murray has agreed to sell the waterworks if they will let Leon go, which they do. The mob ebbs away and I fall onto Leon's lap where he is still kneeling in the dirt. He is all sweaty in the armpits and shaking like a leaf. He hangs onto me like crazy.

"Come on. Let's go home," I say, kissing his shiny head, and I haul him and Rae Ann back to the house.

After that scene, I figure, the city isn't gonna keep Leon around because he will just remind everyone how mad they were at old Murray. And how mad they are that Mr. Murray stuck the city with the cost of digging up all the pipes and reburying them deeper so they won't freeze next time.

We are sitting at our brand-new dining room table, mulling over what to do when Mr. Murray knocks at the door and lets himself into the house like he owns the place, which he does.

"Leon, I am sorry for the trouble. I'm glad I was in town to settle things down," Mr. Murray says, not taking off his hat.

"Thank you, sir. It was a close call, sir," Leon murmurs, staring at his still-trembling hands.

Mr. Murray plunks his fancy leather boot on my new dining room chair, leaving a scuff mark right on the polished wood seat. He leans forward, elbow on his knee, and his cotton trousers pull tight across his fat crotch, which is right in my face. Rae Ann stares up at his hairy nostrils and drools, her babbling baby talk quieted.

"My suggestion to you is to move on out of here, at least until the hostilities die down, and on that note, I am here to make you an offer, Leon."

I look out the window and listen, twisting my new wedding band around my finger.

"I have purchased water rights in California, way down south in San Diego. It's the land of milk and honey," Mr. Murray says, turning to me. "Flowers and orange trees all over the place. Right on the Pacific Ocean! You can take that baby to the beach every day. For that matter, bring your sister along. You'll love it! No more snow!" He pats me on the head and turns back to Leon. "Come run the Cuyamaca Water Company for me. We'll put San Diego on the map."

Mr. Murray stands upright, adjusts his pants, and extends his hand for Leon to shake. "Come with me, son. I need a manager!"

Leon glances over at me and I meet his gaze. Much as Leon and I don't like Mr. Murray, we don't really have a choice. We can't stay here, now that everyone who is anyone in this town just waved their pistol under Leon's nose. And, honestly . . . no more snow? I give Leon a little nod and a shrug as if to say "it's okay with me, but it's your choice."

Leon stretches to his feet and grabs Mr. Murray's hand, giving it a manly double-pump. "Thank you, sir. When do we leave?" And I breathe a sigh of relief.

Story Three:
Natchez 1817

seven

Rae Ann

The kitchen is thick with the scent of boiling oil. I gag over the choking smoke of fried-pork fat griming the air. Breakfast porridge lurches up in the back of my throat and I run outside. It ain't much cooler in the yard, but at least the heat's not pressing so close. Sunlight bakes my face with a fierceness usually reserved for later in the day and when I lift up my hair, gnats dive for my exposed neck. My bowels churn, causing the baby to kick back. Delfa says it's coming any time now, because it ain't rolling over anymore, and them little feet are right up under my ribs. And I have to pee about every two minutes.

Speaking of having to pee, I head over to the outhouse. Mama insisted it be built to match the main house with windows and curtains and a little porch out front. Daddy calls it her "prideful privy." I sling back the wooden door, slap the latch closed, and draw the curtain. Last thing I need is anyone to see this belly sitting in my lap in broad daylight. I flip my skirts up and center myself over the hole, worn smooth by years of endless rubbing. As my stream descends into the darkness below, flies, disturbed by my presence, swirl and buzz, lighting on the tatted lace curtains that frame the view of the meadow stretching to the woods. The outhouse would be a peaceful place to rest if it weren't for the flies and stink. I take my time anyhow and contemplate what's to come.

Daddy ain't spoke to me since I started showing and Mama's main form of communication is the back of her hand. I never said a word, hoping she wouldn't notice and somehow my courses would return and what's growing in my belly would disappear. I prayed for it. But Mama took notice when the seams of my dress split. "Now you've done it, Rae Ann," she said with her hands on her hips and her words cracking sharp as her slap. "Who? Who you been whoring around with?"

"Mama, no. Nobody," I said, sounding sure. "I'm just getting fat lately."

"Lord have mercy, Rae Ann. AM I DAFT? WHO?" she yelled as she walloped my face so hard she left an imprint of her gold wedding band on my cheek.

I didn't see her hand coming because I was hanging my head to hide my shame. Mama can see truth in your eyes. Ears ringing, I said, "No, Mama, no. Nobody. I swear."

She said rumors are gonna fly and I'm not to leave the house, not even for church. Especially not for church. I heard Mama and Daddy talking about me the other day and Daddy said, "Get rid of it." He don't know we already tried. Mama had grabbed me by the hair and dragged me out to Delfa's garden behind the slave cabin, screaming for her to come out there right now. Delfa came running out to me and Mama standing in the dirt beside her patch of tangled weeds. I don't know what all they are, some kind of secret plants for making emmenagogue tea that'll return your courses to you. Delfa knows, though, and she scrambled around picking leaves and yanking up roots while Mama and me watched.

"How long is this going to take, Delfa?" Mama asked, holding me by the arm as if I had somewhere to run to.

"Takes time to brew, won't be ready until afternoon, Ma'am," Delfa answered, not looking at me.

Mama huffed and rolled her eyes, "Lord have mercy. Come get me when it's ready." She yanked me toward the house. "Stay in your room until I come to get you."

I sat in my room for hours that day, waiting. When Delfa's brew was finally ready Mama banged my door open and said, "Come on, now. Get down to the kitchen."

She followed me down and pointed to the little wooden table and chair in the corner where we never sit and Delfa brought me a mug of steaming black liquid.

"Drink it," Mama said, all calm and quiet like she hadn't spent the morning yelling at everybody.

I picked up the mug, cradling the heavy white ceramic in my hands, and sniffed the steam. Little bits of stuff bobbed around in the tea and the sharp scent of herbs filled my nose.

"I said, drink it, Rae Ann," Mama said and slid into the chair opposite me.

There was no avoiding this drink so I gulped it down as fast as the heat would allow, choking on the bitterness while Mama watched. Delfa left us alone in the corner, but I could tell she was watching too, muttering to herself and rubbing that amulet around her neck like she does when she's got something on her mind.

Those herbs worked in my stomach right away and I let out an unladylike belch with a threat of spew behind it. At that moment Mama chose to discuss the upcoming nuptials of Rue and Charlie and the reasons behind them and how, due to those reasons, the wedding would be here in the low country instead of a big affair in Jackson. She carried on talking about the whole thing—dresses and vows and reputations and whatnot—until I couldn't stand it no more. I got up to go outside for some air and Mama said, "Sit down, Rae Ann."

I sat, stomach churning.

"We're gonna make sure that tea don't come back up," she said and carried on about I don't know what. I could not listen as fast as she was talking, yammering on and on. When she ran out of stories, she commenced ordering Delfa to do what she was already doing, like Delfa don't know how to make supper. By this time that tea had moved on to my bowels and I stood up again with certainty.

"Delfa?" Mama looked over at her with one eyebrow raised.

"Yes'm. Okay now." Delfa answered the unspoken question.

Mama nodded at me. "All right then, Rae Ann. Go on."

I was not sure what was supposed to happen, but I barely made it to the outhouse. My guts cramped all through the night. Delfa had to take my chamber pot out three times, checking the pot for courses, but that baby stuck right in there. Delfa tried to help; she's taken care of me all my life. That's why when I turned fifteen last year, Mama gave her to me as a present. I'm to take her with me when I marry—if I ever do—which ain't likely now. Delfa's mine, legal and everything.

I remember that birthday like yesterday. Mama set tables out in the yard and had lanterns strung up in the oaks. Roses on the cake, barbecue, and sweet tea. We sat out under the shade and all the other plantation folks came. Not the poor folks, just the high-cotton neighbors. The boys were sneaking off to the creek with a bottle of whiskey and Rue from the next farm over went with them. I saw her go. And now I'm the low-country slut, which ain't fair because I only done it with Tony once. Anyhow, just as Burley and the boys were getting out the banjos and fiddles, Daddy stood up and raised his preacher's voice, which got everybody's attention. He got them all laughing and then said Mama had an announcement. Mama stood up and said it was her pleasure to give me Delfa as my first slave. Delfa was her girl, they were raised up together, and when Mama married Daddy, she brought her along. Now Mama was handing Delfa down to me as my own. Daddy waved a parchment around over his head and said for me to come sign. I cain't read the words, but I can dip a quill and make an X, which I did with only a little bit of splotching. And then Mama and Daddy looked so proud and I felt grown. They had high hopes for me.

Mama called Delfa out of the kitchen and she came out standing in front of everyone with her hands wrapped up in her apron, looking down.

Mama said, "Delfa, you belong to Miss Rae Ann now."

And Delfa nodded without looking up. And then Mama said, show her who's boss, and she turned to Delfa's boy Tony and said, "Go get me the whip, boy," and he did.

And I stepped up and took the whip outta Mama's hand.

"Hold on, now. You don't want to wreck her dress. Tell Delfa to pull it down, Rae Ann." With hands on her hips, she said, "You act like you ain't never seen this done before."

And I told Delfa to pull her dress down to her waist and everybody laughed again. I thought they were laughing at me and that made me mad, so I said to her I said, "Do it!" and cracked the whip against the ground like Mama does. The slick leather handle warm in my grip. I could see Delfa's eyes watering, but she undid her buttons and pulled her top down by the neck and her sleeves turned inside out and her breasts shone in the sun, glistening sweat running down between 'em.

The party guests hooped and hollered and said, "Go on, Rae Ann, show her now."

Delfa curled her arms over her exposed skin and hunched forward as I raised the whip and cracked it down on her back. The braided leather hissed past my ear. A red welt raised up on Delfa's back.

"Like you mean it, Rae Ann," Mama ordered.

And the crowd joined in, urging me on. I raised the whip again and brought it down harder this time and Delfa's brown skin split across her backbone. A trickle of blood ran down over her ribs and the whoops of my party guests roared in my ears and I couldn't stop until Daddy laughed and said, "That's enough now, baby. She ain't worth nothing dead." And Delfa crumpled into the dirt.

Burley started up the music and the boys passed the bottle out in the open now and everybody got loose. They all stayed way into dark and Daddy twirled me around, handing me off to the boys on the turns. I saw Rue slip off again with Charlie this time, back down toward the creek. While I was watching, I saw Daddy headed to the slave cabins with Rue's pa. I saw Mama see him go, her mouth set grim. Me and the high-cotton girls laughed about Rue and her shenanigans, and they admired the red callous marks on my palms from gripping the whip and said how that must-a hurt my soft hands. I said yes it did and also my shoulder was sore from working it so hard, playing up my wincing. That was the last time they came over. I guess they're all laughing about me now.

Try as I might, I cain't spend all day in the privy, so I follow the path through the scratch weeds down to the creek, belly leading the way. Delfa says I ain't all that big, but Mama says I'm too big to hide my sin and the Lord knows anyway. Along this path is where me and Tony used to meet up. We are the same age and been running around together ever since we could walk—and even now when he ain't working—just like our mamas did when they were kids.

Tony always had a way of making me laugh, and I snuck sweet treats out of the house for him to eat. After the beating I gave his mama, he stopped talking to me, which he got no right to do, so I followed him outside one evening. He was doing the house chores for Delfa, chopping wood for the next day and whatnot. Ever since he turned fifteen, just before I did, his muscles been growing muscles and he takes on more and more of the house chores for Delfa, after he's done in the fields.

Anyhow, I followed him as he carried the buckets out to the well and said, "Hey, what's stuck in your craw?"

And he said, "I ain't got no problem, Miss Rae Ann. What you need?"

And I mimicked him and said, "What I neeeeed, Mr. Anthony, is for you to talk to me right now."

"I ain't got nothing to say." He cranked the well handle.

"Come down to the creek with me," I said, not asking. "Leave them buckets."

"Mama waiting for the water, Miss."

"I said leave them buckets and come with me now."

Tony stood up straight and looked down at me with an expression I couldn't read.

"Yes ma'am."

I ran ahead thinking he'd chase me like he used to, but he don't. We got down to the creek bed and I pulled him into the water, wading upstream until we got to our old hideout, a big, flat slab of rock surrounded by sweetshrub. I pushed him down on the rock and grabbed his shoulders. "I know you mad I whupped your mama. You know I had to do it. She mine now."

"Maybe you'll beat me too."

"Only if you don't stop sulkin'."

I climbed onto his legs, running my hands over his shoulders. He finally looked into my eyes.

One thing led to another and here we are. Now I know what Rue was sneaking around with Charlie for and I don't blame her. Don't nobody know Tony the father of this baby yet. I won't tell. I cain't. If it was a local boy, we'd have to get married like Rue and Charlie are doing. But I can't marry Tony or have his baby either, so I got no idea what is to come of this. I am afeared for my life and Tony's too.

The creek is summertime low, but there's enough water to cover my feet. So I sit on the smooth rock and strip off my shoes and stockings, sinking my swollen feet below the surface. Mosquitoes whine against my face and the hard surface of the rock pushes against my nethers, pushing my belly up against my lungs and I cain't catch air. I ain't got room for everything going on inside me, there ain't no place for it all. Water skimmers cross over my feet and then I see a cottonmouth slither downstream and that's my sign to go. I heave upright, my wet feet dripping on the rock, but then a sharp crack of pain and my feet are wetter than they were.

Sweet Jesus, what is happening? Another stab and a gush, and I know I better get myself back to the house. I hobble as quick as I can up the path, wet skirts clinging to my legs, and stop to heave bile into the weeds as the pain comes again.

"Delfaaaaaaa," I holler as I get to the yard, sobbing through my breath, my legs shaking. She comes running out to get me and holds me up as we stumble to the house.

"Baby coming, Miss Rae Ann. You better get to bed."

She starts barking orders to the house girl Tansy and her daughter Penny Royal to fetch this and that.

"Where's Mama?" I whimper as another pain racks my body.

"Shshshshhhhh, she comin'. Here, put this on." Delfa retrieves my nightgown from under my pillow. "Get this dress off." She undoes my buttons and pulls my bodice down by the neck, the sleeves turn inside out, my breasts showing. Delfa lifts my nightgown over my head as my dress falls to the floor.

"Get that dress off the floor, Delfa!" I snap.

"Yes, ma'am. I got it, Miss." She scoops up my dress, turns it right side out, and hangs it up where it belongs.

"I need water. Get me water," I pant.

"Yes, ma'am, water coming, Miss." Delfa turns and hollers, "Penny Royal, hurry up with that water, now."

She directs Tansy to pull the covers off the bed without dragging them on the floor and spread an extra sheet and cotton towels down.

"Lie down, you just lay back and let me see what's what," she says as she eases me back onto the bed.

Delfa spreads another sheet over my legs. I feel her dry, rough hands peel my knickers off.

"Delfa!" I yell. "What in the world are you doing?"

"Where you think this baby comin' out at, Miss?" she asks.

My chest clutches and my breath becomes shallow as another pain shoots through me and I realize I hadn't thought about which way the baby was gonna arrive. I ain't never seen a birth except for the goats one time. *Dear Lord, have mercy.*

Delfa peers under the sheet and feels around, prodding and poking in the same place where Tony put it in. *That's where the baby will come out, I reckon. Busy place. Like a beehive with all this comin' and going down there.*

"That hurts like it don't want to, Delfa. What are you doing to me?"

"All right, Miss. If you lucky this baby'll come quick. The head ain't too far up."

Thank the Lord for Delfa; she delivers all the babies around here. Someone over yonder wanted to borrow her awhile back for delivery, but I said no and they had to abide by it because Delfa is mine, I cain't do without her even for a day. Mama said I was going to cause trouble with my selfishness, but it's my say.

Another pain comes and I hear Mama's boots in the hall. She peeks her head in and glares at me. She pulls her head back and I hear her tell Daddy, "It's time."

"What color is it?" I hear him say from the hall.

"Hush, Leon. I don't know yet. Delfa is gonna get her to tell. Soon now."

Daddy mumbled something to her and Mama said, "Get on out of here, Leon. I'll tell you when it's over. Go on." I hear the thud of his footsteps down the stairs.

This time, the pain barely breaks before it starts again and I hear a wail as if from another place, but it was me, sounding like that mama goat. Despite having spent the morning daydreaming in the outhouse, I feel hot feces bulge out and the acrid tang telling me I shit the bed. Nobody told me that was going to happen.

And Delfa says, "Tell me now, Miss."

I pant, "Huh?"

"Who this baby's daddy? You tell me now."

The pressure between my legs feels like a steam engine and I wail again.

"Tell me now, Miss, or this pain won't never stop."

"No, I cain't, Delfa. Weren't nobody."

"You got to tell me now, Miss. Every baby has a daddy. Who was it?"

And the pain again. And again.

"Tell me, Miss, or your Daddy coming in here with the wrath-a God on his shoulders," Delfa warns, leaning into me like she's trying to push that baby back up inside me. Her eyes have gone black and that strange brass amulet on a leather cord she always wears hangs over my belly, twisted metal rings shaped like fingers dangling between me and her, swinging in and out of my vision, over my belly and back between my legs. I feel like I am going to explode as the pain comes again, pushing against Delfa's hands.

"Tony, it was Tony," I whisper, squinching my eyes shut and twisting a handful of sweaty sheets as bile pours out of me and down the side of the bed.

Delfa goes still. Her breath titches and she releases the pressure on me.

"Please don't tell Daddy. Please, Delfa."

She turns her attention to whatever is happening under the sheet, her hands on my knees. "Bear down, Miss," Delfa croaks like something's in her throat. "You almost there. Push now."

Mama strides into the room and stands between me and Delfa, her back to me, not looking at me at all. She murmurs something I cain't hear and I see Delfa nod. Mama moves in so her head and shoulders block Delfa's face from me as she grips onto my bent knees, pulling them apart. The sheet over my legs is stretched and held tight so I cannot see past my heaving belly.

Then pressure like I cain't tell overcomes me and I squeeze my eyes shut again. "Push now," I hear Delfa holler from far away. I wail as great release comes in a rush and in the middle of it all I hear a small, muffled mew like a kitten under the floorboards.

Then, silence.

I hear Mama stomp out with her stern boots and swirl of skirts and I open my eyes.

"Mamaaaaaa?" I call out, but she doesn't come back.

Tansy bustles in with another stack of rags.

"Where is it? Lemme see it," I say, my voice creaking out.

"Miss Rae Ann, honey, baby didn't make it. It were stillborn," Delfa murmurs.

"What? *What!?*" Confusion and panicked sobs overtake me. "What happened? *Why?*" I babble.

"Only the Lord knows why, Miss," Delfa mumbles as she wipes my legs. "It ain't never took a breath. Hold still, the rest coming out."

"But what was it, where is it?" I shriek as another contraction rips through me and something else slithers out.

"It all out now, Miss. All done. Don't matter what it was, it with Jesus now. Better this way. You rest now, hear?" Delfa says and walks out, leaving me alone.

Delfa

When Miss Rae Ann said my boy's name, the room went dark. I knew it but didn't want to let myself know. Rebecca's shadow fell across the sheet and I nodded to her. She hissed like a snake right in my face. "Don't let it take a breath," she said, and I could smell the sourness of her fear. I nodded again and kept my eyes on the emerging crown of black hair between Rae Ann's legs. My grand-baby for whom there was no hope. I remembered when my sister was auctioned off to another family to another place far away from me. I wanted nothing more than to go with her, but instead I was tethered to the sister I did not claim as she was also sent away. Sent here. Here we are, another incestuous tangle of abom-inations from which there is no escape, except for this little one whose head is in my hands. Rebecca reaches down quick as light-ning to grab its face. The pudgy little body that follows is covered all over with hair almost like fur. I have never seen anything like it. Rebecca swoops away with him, white swaths of cotton swad-dling trailing behind her sharp boots. I turn back to the matter at hand, but instead of the afterbirth I expect to catch, a tiny body no bigger than a teacup and slippery as an eel slithers out of Rae Ann into my hands. The body doesn't move. Rae Ann hollers again as the gush of fluid and afterbirth follows. I leave the tiny one in the bucket under the rest. No matter now.

Rebecca

I rock back and forth on the porch as the afternoon light bakes the earth. It's so hot the air glitters. I am waiting for Delfa's brew to take hold of my daughter. Hopefully it will set Rae Ann's courses right and I won't have to tell Leon. If it is early enough, Rae Ann won't have any lasting damage and her future husband will never be able to tell she's already tainted, Lord willing. Water under the bridge, as they say. I am concerned I have left the pregnancy too late, but at least we can hope for a stillbirth, early and small so maybe Rae Ann won't stretch out.

If Anthony is that baby's daddy, what on earth will we do with it? A Black baby with a white mama is born free. I could likely get a slaver to take it downriver and tell 'em it's Tansy's baby. Or even Penny Royal's, she is about old enough. Lord knows we sold off babies before. Rae Ann don't have to know anything, but I need Leon to make a legal sale—though because of his emotional nature, I would rather he not be involved. I should have sent her to Delfa as soon as I suspected, but I could not believe Rae Ann could be this stupid. I should have known letting her run around with that boy would lead to trouble. Being raised together, they've always been thick as thieves.

If Rae Ann has the smarts to name a church boy—though Lord knows she don't—we can marry her off and get her outta here before the backlash starts. If word gets around that she had a Black baby, Leon'll get shoved out of the church, and then what? Our name'll be mud, that's what. Outcasts. Nothing like a wayward daughter to bring a good man down. We'll lose the church and likely the farm too, and before you know it, Rae Ann will be living down in the swamp like a slattern, having a baby with whoever comes along. Leon and I will be as poor as church mice. No thank you. Everything we built for the last twenty years—gone overnight. We're too old to start over in another backwater parish. Lord knows there's no forgiveness in the body of Christ.

Rocking and twisting my wedding band around my finger until it's red-hot, I watch crows squawking at each other in the oak trees. I consider the idea that Anthony forced himself on Rae Ann, but no—that boy is as mild-mannered as they come. I do not believe I can convince anyone of Anthony being the culprit, not even myself.

If word gets out, Rae Ann won't ever find a husband of any repute. The only way to keep Leon in the ministry, hang on to this property, and quell the rumors is to marry Rae Ann off to someone who'll take her. An older gentleman from elsewhere, perhaps. That's the next problem, though. Right now, I have to decide what happens to this baby. From my rocker, I watch a crow surprise a red-breasted robin, holding it down in the grass with its talons, pecking at its head while the robin lets out strangled, panicked chirps. When the robin stops struggling, the crow flies off with the limp body of its victim in its yellow beak.

I'd best take matters in hand and tell Leon sooner rather than later. I snap up out of the rocker and head into the cool shade of the house. Leon'll see it my way, I'll make sure of that. I remember when we first got married and he brought me here, just me and Delfa. Me and Delfa the same age, grown up together just like Rae Ann and Anthony. She was given to me on my fifteenth birthday and she's been mine ever since, until I bequeathed her to Rae Ann.

First day in this house after we got married, we were settling in, Delfa cooking up breakfast, and Leon comes up behind her and grabs her around the neck, just like he did me when we were courting. And he said, "Looks like I got two for one." He didn't know I was in the doorway. I shrank back so he wouldn't see me and I watched him run his hands around Delfa's waist. I tiptoed backward down the hall and made loud footsteps coming forward so he would hear me coming and he slipped out the back in a hurry.

By the time I had Rae Ann a year later, Delfa already had Anthony. I didn't ever ask but our babies sure looked mighty similar, despite being different colors. We had to bring on Tansy at that point because Delfa had two babies to feed and couldn't keep up alone. It all worked out as Anthony added to my ownings, not Leon's, and I had me a wet nurse. Me and Delfa was tense after that, and I learnt quick to shackle her up whenever Leon was around, but that was years past now and he moved on to others long ago. Ever since Delfa put that herb garden in behind the quarters, there ain't been no more white babies born on this farm. No thanks to Leon.

I walk slowly down the hall to Leon's study where he writes his sermons, rehearsing my approach. He's in there now, leaning back in his leather chair while fan blades slice shadows across his mahogany desk, Bible spread before him. His eyes closed, contemplating God's word with a little snooze.

"Leon, I need a word." I settle down on his knee and wrap my arm around his collar. Kiss him on the cheek real soft to gentle him up. He wakes up with a little grunt.

"What do you need, Rebecca," Leon asks. "I was lost in prayer."

"We have a situation."

"Do we now? And what might that be?"

"Our little Rae Ann seems to have got herself into some trouble."

"Lord have mercy. What?"

"She's with child. There's no denying it. Ain't likely another virgin birth."

"Likely not. Who is the father? That Charlie boy?" Leon groans and rubs his eyes.

"Nooo . . . she won't say whose. I don't know for certain and I did question her most severely," I defend, thinking back to my handprints on Rae Ann's face. "I cain't get it out of her yet, but there's ways. I will find out. Don't you worry about that. If it's a church boy, they'll have to marry. If it's who I suspect, she's ruint."

"Who do you suspect?"

"Delfa's boy, Anthony."

"Good Lord, Rae Ann has never had a lick of sense," he says, shaking his head. "The Devil has taken hold of her feeble mind."

"Anyhow, at this point we need to have a plan. I thought on sending her to Cousin Sarah's in Jackson for a spell, if she can keep quiet about it."

"You're exactly right, Rebecca. We'll either marry her off or send her to Sarah for a time, depending." Leon squeezes his thick arm around my middle and gives me a little shake, like he does. "Perhaps find a suitable husband in Jackson who hasn't heard the rumors. Hey now, doesn't Sarah have an older brother with a reputation? That Bubba fellow? Perhaps he can be inclined to take her off our hands after she's healed up," Leon says, rubbing the smooth mahogany edge of his desk.

"Oh Leon, that's a wonderful idea. Cousin Bubba! He needs a wife to settle him down and Lord knows he ain't in a position to be particular. I knew you would know what to do," I say, all sweet relief, and slide off his lap, giving his thigh a little squeeze as I go.

"I'll take care of Anthony, either way." Leon sighs. "What in the world will you do with the infant?"

"Well, there's not much chance it will survive with Rae Ann being so young," I tell Leon. This is a lie he pretends to believe, knowing full well fifteen-year-olds have babies all the time. Perhaps he forgot that's how old Tansy was when she had Penny Royal. But likely he never thought about it. The fewer people knowing the fate of this baby the better, and that includes Leon.

"I trust your judgment on this, Rebecca," Leon says and turns back to his Bible.

I quick-step out of his office and down the hall to the kitchen to seek out Delfa. She stands at the biscuit box, up to her elbows in dough, punching and turning. The smell of ripe yeast makes my mouth water.

"Listen here, Delfa. When Rae Ann's pains come, you tell me right away so's if your emmenagogue doesn't work, I can be right there."

"Yes'm," Delfa nods and rolls the dough.

"Right. Look at me. She has to confess to the father of this child. You find out, understand?"

"Yes'm."

"Don't you give me that blank look. Do you understand me?" I hiss at her.

"Yes'm, I hear you." She nods, turning the dough in her hands.

"Do not call me too late."

I don't explain what I am planning. I don't tell anyone at all.

When Rae Ann's pains start, Delfa helps her into the house all wet and squalling, and I am on hand to hear. I hang back to give the girls time to get Rae Ann settled in the bed and let Delfa do her business. Leon hears the commotion and comes to stick his nose in. I shoo him away. That's all I need . . . him lurking around right now.

I keep my ear to the crack in the door while Delfa questions Rae Ann and I hear her confession. My heart about sinks into my stomach, but I did expect that name. I lean against the wall to catch my breath listening to Rae Ann's animal sounds. I know it's time, so I gather my will and enter the room, leaning on her legs, positioning myself so Rae Ann can't see what comes out of her or what I am about to do. She will thank me someday.

A scalp of wet black curls emerges from between her legs, and then a scrunched-up little blue face. I reach down with my hanky and squeeze its nose, stifling its first cry. I hang onto that face as the rest of its body slips out into Delfa's hands, blood and water raining into the bucket between her feet. I grab the cloth off Delfa's lap and pull it around the baby's neck while Delfa ties off the cord. As soon as she snips it with the kitchen shears, I have that little body wrapped in cotton and held to my breast, and swoop out of the room, never looking back at Rae Ann.

I fly, fly through the kitchen and out the back door with a death grip on that baby's face, its little body limp and still in my arms. It never moved, but I can't take a chance on it catching a breath. The will to live is strong. I grab up the trailing cotton swaddling and wrap and wrap as tightly as I can with one hand, running down the trail behind the slave quarters and into the woods.

Brambles catch my skirts as the path narrows. Splashing across the shallow creek up the far bank and further into the forest, I know where I am going even though the path is nothing more than a deer trail now. There is a spot a little farther on where the forest floor is soft and covered with pine needles. I snuck out here weeks ago, dug a hole, and left the shovel. Our farmhand beat one of the slaves for that missing shovel.

The grave appears before me, and I am running pell-mell and didn't realize it was coming up so fast. I almost trip into it. I stand at the edge of the sorry little hole I dug, sweating and gulping for air. I kneel beside the open grave, doubting it is deep enough. The bundle in my arms is no longer warm. I tighten the swaddling around and around its body and lay it on the crumbling earth at the bottom of the pit.

Shaking, I rise to my feet and grasp the shovel from beside the tree, piling dirt, rocks, pinecones, and needles into the hole as fast as I can. When the earth is turned onto the bundle and the hole is full, I climb onto the soft mound and stomp it level as best I can. *What is to stop a critter from digging this grave up?* I wonder. The creek is too far away to haul a rock big enough to matter. Also, I do not want to mark the spot. I will have to take this chance. I throw the shovel as far as I can back into the trees.

I slowly walk back down the path to gather myself. When I get to the creek's far edge, I take stock. My dress has ungodly splatters on it and my hands are covered with dirt, packed in under my fingernails. I kneel on the flat rock under the sweetshrub and wash my hands, digging the dirt from under my nails with a thorn. There's nothing can be done about my dress. As I take a moment to rest, I glimpse a piece of white cloth under the sweetshrub and pull out a stocking that can only be Rae Ann's. I run it through my fingers and wrap it around and around my wrist until my hand swells and turns blood-red, feeling my own throbbing pulse in my fingertips.

Rae Ann

I sit on the edge of the bed, swinging my legs and dragging my toes over the floorboards. For two weeks I been laid up and won't nobody talk to me. Mama and Daddy come and go but don't never poke their heads into my room even to say good morning. Tansy bustles in and out with clean cottons and food trays. Delfa comes in to help me bind up my breasts so's the milk will stop coming. As soon as she unwraps the binding, stinking of sour milk and sweat, I feel that tingle starting up in my armpits and I know my breasts ain't figured out yet that there's no baby to feed.

"It'll stop soon," Delfa says. "Time to get up and outta the bedroom. Your mama says no more laying around." Then she walks out.

Tansy never did come with dinner, so I guess that's it then. I heave myself to my feet, my stomach still slack and loose from where the baby was. Delfa says that'll tighten up again because I'm young and the baby didn't grow right, so it wasn't very big. It felt big enough to me when it was in there, but what do I know. At least the bleeding is slowing down now.

I wander out to the kitchen yard where little Penny Royal, Tansy's girl, sits on a stump shelling peas.

"Where's Tony at?" I ask.

Without breaking rhythm, Penny Royal says, "He gone, Miss."

"Gone where?"

"Your pa took him to auction while you was laid up, Miss. Been gone two weeks now."

I stare down at Penny Royal's white cotton bonnet, her tight braids poking out from underneath the edges. Watch her fingers snap a pod and her thumb run through it, peas dribbling into the bowl between her knees. Empty peapod drops in the bucket at her feet. Again. *Snap, zip, plink.* Crickets chirp in the weeds behind the slave cabin. Sparrows flit over the garden as the late afternoon sun bakes end-of-summer ironweed. I sit down on the other stump next to Penny Royal, mesmerized by the rhythm of her hands, her slim fingers. *Snap, zip, plink.* Her wrists twisting in opposite motion, dancing with the sound of falling peas. Her wrist bones bulge from under the edge of her sleeves, just like mine do. I rub the rounded bone that juts up from my wrist, like a robin's egg under my skin. I ain't never seen anybody else's bones look like that, just me and Penny Royal. And Daddy's.

I lean over to grab a peapod, split the pod, and empty the green pearls into my mouth, sweet and earthy on my tongue. Toss the pod on the ground.

Delfa opens the kitchen screen door with her hip, hands gripping a skillet, and calls across the yard, "Miss Rae Ann, your mama says your daddy wants to see you in his study right away."

"Right now? Why?"

"I don't know why, Miss. Right away, yes'm," Delfa says, letting the screen door slap back into place.

My stomach lurches. I ain't never been called into Daddy's study before. He writes his sermons in there and everybody knows not to interrupt. I step slowly through the kitchen and down the hall, feeling dread, like something behind that door might be the end of me. His heavy mahogany door is ajar and I rap my knuckles on the carved panel.

"Daddy?" I peek in through the crack.

He is sitting behind the desk with papers all spread out in front of him. I asked him once to show me how to read, back when I was little enough to run in and climb on his lap. He said no need for me to know how to read; it's just something men need for business and Bible reading. He said he would tell me what I need to know.

He looks up over the top of his spectacles and clears his throat like I am interrupting, "Come in, Rae Ann, and shut the door behind you."

I do so and stand before him, unsure if I should sit or not.

"Sit down, Rae Ann," Daddy said, thumbing through the Bible.

"Yessir," I say and sit, my quivering knees quick to give in.

Daddy sets his open Bible on the desk and reads, "Train up a child in the way he should go; even when he is old he will not depart from it."

He glares at me over his spectacles.

"Proverbs 22:6."

Daddy leans back in his chair and sighs. He purses his lips and folds his hands over his paunch belly. "Rae Ann, recent events have left me sorely disappointed in you."

Sunlight slants through the dark wood of his window shutters, gleaming on the high polish of his desk.

"Do you not realize the repercussions of your actions?"

"I'm sorry, Daddy," I whisper.

"You're sorry? Are you so dimwitted as to believe that your carelessness, your absolute disregard for my position in the church would go unnoticed? Do you care for no one but your-self?" he spits.

I open my mouth to speak, but he carries on, winding up as if his desk was the pulpit on Sunday morning.

"Your mother's heart is broken to see you become a loose woman after all her care and teaching. You've gone and rejected the righteous path laid out before you. How can I minister to hea-thens when my own daughter is a harlot? If my reputation is ruined by you and I am unable to minister, the unsaved folks in this community—the fate of their souls—are on your conscience. You will have literal blood and burning flesh on your hands. Do you understand that, Rae Ann?"

I nod my head, barely breathing, staring at his fat hands planted on the desk, his bulging wrist bones poking out from un-der his cuffs.

"Your mother and I could well lose this very land that feeds us, and then where will we go? Did you think of that while you were indulging in the pleasures of the flesh? Did you, Rae Ann?"

Tears gather in my throat and my cheeks flame with hot shame. I stutter, "No, sir."

"Shut your mouth. You will leave in the morning to go to Cousin Sarah's house in Jackson. She has generously agreed to look after you. As you know, most folks around here think you've already gone visiting, and, indeed, now you will be."

"All the way to Jackson? Tomorrow? For how long?" I whisper.

Daddy returned his attention to his Bible.

"We'll see."

He doesn't look up again and I deduce my dismissal. I walk back down the hall as if in a dream and up the stairs to my bed-room. The travel trunk is set in the middle of the floor, lid up. Inside, neatly folded, are all of my clothes. Delfa is just laying a shawl across the top of the stacks and tucking it neatly between the clothing and sides of the case.

"You're coming with me, Delfa. You're mine, now."

"No, Miss, I am not allowed. Your mama says I'm to stay here."

"But you're mine," I protest, unable to comprehend the injustice. Delfa does not answer.

"Then who is taking me to Jackson?" I whisper.

"Old Tom."

"But I mean who is going with me? Is Mama coming along?"

"Not to my knowledge, Miss. I'll be getting you up real early in the morning. Y'all leaving while it still dark. Maybe you want to rest while you can," Delfa says as she walks out.

The room spins. I sink onto the bed and curl around myself.

Delfa raps on my bedroom door while I'm dead asleep at three o'clock in the morning. I stir as she comes on in and jiggles my shoulder. "Get up, Miss Rae Ann. Time to go, come on now."

"Mrff," I groan, body unresponsive until the memory of why I am getting up so early returns. A wild flutter of panic wakes my limbs and bladder and I pull myself from under the sheets and squat over the chamber pot. The trunk with all my clothes is already gone.

"Delfa, what about my nightgown? You gotta put it in the trunk."

"Sorry, Miss, your trunk is in the buggy already. Your mama said to pack your other one and just leave that one here for rags."

"But I hate that one, I only like this one. That other one itches me."

"I'm sorry, Miss. Old Tom ready to go down there. Let's change out your bindings and courses quick now and get you into your dress," Delfa says as she holds out my shift from yesterday.

She unwraps and rewraps my breasts, hands me fresh course rags to catch the last rusty discharge of birthing blood, and dresses me like a rag doll while I hardly know what is happening. I am barely awake, but a pounding deep in my head has begun. I follow Delfa down the stairs and out the front door where Old Tom and the horses and buggy are waiting under the low-hanging, full moon, bright as day. Neither Mama nor Daddy are there to say goodbye.

Delfa hands me a lunch pail and says, "Take care, now, Miss."

"Bye, Delfa," I say as Old Tom helps me into the buggy without looking at me.

He climbs up top, clicks his tongue, and snaps the reins on the horses' backs. I lean to the window to wave goodbye to Delfa, but she is already back in the house. I settle back on the leather seat, dank night air closing in around me. As the horses pick up speed, bright moonlight filters through the trees, their wild shadows like dancing witches on the sides of the road. I know the shadows are only shadows, but it sure feels like they are reaching out for me. Soft thunder of the horses' hooves and swaying of the buggy lull me as we move through the night.

I wake to find a thin string of drool soaking into my bodice, my neck stiff and sore from lolling about unrestrained. Morning light seeps into the sky, just visible above the tree line. We are on the Natchez Trace to Jackson, a trail closed in on both sides by forest and swamp. I have made this journey to Cousin Sarah's before, the ninety miles of soft road discouraging frequent travel. At the pace we are going, I figure we will be there by midafternoon, allowing for stops. Speaking of which, I holler, "Hey Tom! When we stopping?"

"Not yet, Miss Rae Ann," he calls back. "Not until we can see what we doin'."

I guess I'll hold it, then. I fumble in the pail Delfa gave me and pull out a packet of cornbread in waxed paper. Stick my hand back in for something more but that's all there is. Punishment pursues me even in the lunch pail. I take a nibble and put the bread back in its wrapper. *As hungry as I am, I will be hungrier later*, I think as the pounding in my head resumes. I stick my head out the window for air.

The Natchez Trace is a tunnel of green, close and humid, suffocating. The higher the sun climbs, the hotter and more still the air becomes between the endless trees. Wild turkeys squawk and flap in the road to avoid the oncoming horses. Flies, gnats, and mosquitoes drone in and out the window and I am drowsy again, alone. Night shadows have dissipated, but the ghosts of trees still reach for me. A vulture clutches the moss-covered branch of a cypress tree; a long white strand of something hangs from its curved beak.

Eventually, we stop to water the horses at a creek running close to the road. The worn-out patch of dirt tells me we aren't the first ones there. I climb down out of the buggy, stiff-legged and sore, before Old Tom can help me down. I step my way across the limestone by the stream looking for privacy.

"We got to move on quick now," Old Tom says. "Don't wander too far, please, Miss. There are likely Kaintucks about."

I know all about the Kaintucks, those ragtag men who raft wares down the Mississippi River from up North to our port in Natchez or on down to New Orleans. They sell off their goods and their flatboats too, and walk the Trace back home, only to do it all again. They're a wild bunch, everybody knows to steer clear of 'em and let 'em pass on through. I don't rightly know what might happen if we were to encounter them deep on the Trace, miles away from nowhere. I wonder how Mama and Daddy didn't think of that when they sent me out here with nobody but Old Tom. I hurry about my business and climb up into the buggy. I pull out my cornbread. I can't wait to eat any longer. The dull pounding in my head is a throbbing vise. We're back on our way, slower now, as the horses are tired. I am torn between wanting to get there and dreading arrival, as I have no fond memories of Cousin Sarah.

Cousin Sarah is Mama's first cousin from the side of the family with all the money. Mama said her daddy and Sarah's daddy were brothers and had fishing boats up in Massachusetts, and that's how Mama got the money to start the farm in Natchez and the church too. It weren't Daddy's money at all, but don't say that in front of him. Anyhow, the only times I been to Cousin Sarah's she looks down her nose and talks sharp. I heard her snap at Mama one time about why did she marry a no-good, smooth-talking preacher who can't earn a dime and Mama got mad and said what do you know about it? Nobody ever wanted to marry you anyway because you are so ugly and sharp-tongued. And then Mama and Cousin Sarah weren't speaking for a day and a half.

Hours later, feeling half-dead from the heat and stomach-sick from the constant sway of the buggy, we pull up to Cousin Sarah's house, a big white two-story with wrought iron gates out front and a packed dirt drive. I stumble out of the buggy and stand looking at the surroundings, all clean and green. Their house help come out to show Old Tom where to go and usher me inside. Cousin Sarah sails into the front hall.

"Hey Rae Ann, I just got your mama's note the other day. Come on in. You must be tired."

"Yes, ma'am, I am," I say, grateful for a welcome.

"Well, you make yourself at home. The girls will see to you."
She sweeps past me with a quick pat on the shoulder and the
house girl takes me to the kitchen.

I am starving by now and ask for a bite, so they say, of course,
sugar, and make me a plate of cold beans and cornbread. They
show me to my room at the back of the house, small, simple, and
plain, likely one of the housemaid's rooms not in use right now,
with my trunk already in it. I feel sure it is a mistake and I'm just
about to say so when Cousin Sarah reappears and says, "You'll
sleep here until we get your situation sorted out."

"Ma'am? What do you mean, ma'am? What's my situation?" I
ask.

"Your *situation*, Rae Ann, is that you are ruint in the eyes of
God and have brought shame to this family. Tainted and unwor-
thy of a godly husband," Cousin Sarah barks with her hands on
her hips. "The Bible says, 'And the daughter of any priest, if she
profane herself by playing the whore, she profaneth her father:
she shall be burnt with fire.' Leviticus 21:9. You can consider
yourself fortunate to be taken in. I won't have your ingratitude
nor one ounce of sass out of your mouth. While you're here, you
will do as I say. You hear me?" Cousin Sarah's eyes burn through
me.

"Yes, Ma'am," I mumble.

"Yes, ma'am *what*, Rae Ann?" she mocks.

"Yes, ma'am, thank you, ma'am," I stutter, unsure of the correct response.

"Hmpf." Cousin Sarah rolls her eyes. "Dinner is at eight. Get
cleaned up. Cousin Bubba will be here." She swirls back out and
stomps through the kitchen. From behind the bedroom wall, her
footsteps sound exactly like Mama's. Cousin Sarah's brother,

Bubba, is a bachelor everybody talks about in whispers. I have never met him.

The washbowl in the corner of my room has water with only a few floating fruit flies in it, so I dip my hands in and wipe my face. There isn't a towel of any kind, so I use the hem of my shift to dry off. I step out of my room cautiously and into the kitchen. The house girls are there already making dinner. Delicious smells fill the air and my stomach growls. However, I have more immediate needs. "I need one-a y'all to help me with something," I say to the house girls.

"Sure, Miss, whatchu need?" the younger one asks nervously.

"I'm having my courses and I need some fresh linens," I say, straightening my shoulders up. The young one rushes to help me out, but the other one slips out toward the sitting room.

A minute later, Cousin Sarah comes stomping back in and shoves me backward to my room. "You are not to ask *my help* for anything, do you understand? You will deal with *your situation* as best you can. *Hear?*"

"Yes, ma'am." I quiver.

Cousin Sarah slams the door. This time it liked to stop my heart, and I squat to peel away the cotton wrapping where it is stuck to my skin with a dried crust of blood. My flow has greatly decreased and the thought of finding a basin, pumping water, taking it to my bedroom or the outhouse, attempting to wipe up, and then digging through my trunk on the off-chance Delfa packed course cottons is entirely too much. I wrap my used cottons into a ball and shove them under the bed. With any luck, I won't bleed anymore tonight.

A rap at the door and the younger house girl pokes her head in. "Ma'am says you're to come help with dinner, Miss."

Help with dinner? Help how?

I go to the kitchen and the older girl hands me a stack of plates and says to set the table. I never set a table in my life. I walk into the dining room, the plates clattering in my shaking grip. I set them down at each place and wonder if one is for me.

Cousin Sarah sidles up behind me, straightening plates. "If you're ever going to have a household of any kind, you'd best learn a thing or two about how to run one. You've been spoilt beyond belief, living out there in the swamp with nary a responsibility. Help the girls bring out the food, then sit in that spot right there," she orders, pointing to a straight-backed chair to the left of the head of the table.

"Yes, Ma'am. Thank you, Ma'am," I stammer. At least I get to eat.

Once pitchers of sweet tea and platters heaped with fried catfish, ham, cornbread, pickled vegetables, greens, and peas are set on the table, I sit where Cousin Sarah tells me to.

"Lord have mercy, your manners are atrocious," she says. "Get up and wait for your elders." She turns to Cousin Bubba, standing in the doorway. "We have a lot of work to do, I'm afraid."

He smirks and swirls a crystal tumbler of amber liquid.

"Cousin Bubba, please honor us by taking the head of the table." Cousin Sarah gestures to his seat.

"Wouldn't care to," he says as he lowers himself into the armchair at the end of the table. He says the blessing and the house girls rush to serve and back quickly away, avoiding eye contact with Cousin Bubba, even though he seems to be trying to get their attention. His eyes rake over them both, then he turns his attention to me, lifting his empty glass in my direction and giving it a little shake.

"Rae Ann, hop up and get your Cousin Bubba another drink," Cousin Sarah orders.

I startle at the request, but shakily take his glass to the sideboard. I have seen whiskey poured more times than I can count but have never lifted the crystal decanter myself. It is heavy and slippery in my sweaty hand and I drip whiskey onto the silver tray.

"Careful, now," Cousin Bubba says with a smirk.

I return his glass to him, sliding it across the white tablecloth toward his hand. I glance up to see if I can return to my chair and see his soft, full lips pulled into a smile below a calculating squint. Cousin Bubba sips his whiskey and reaches under the table to adjust himself.

Story Four:
Marblehead Harbor 1677

Delfa

I cannot resist the moonlight. The pull of darkness lures me to the water's edge, the only sound the soft lapping of waves sliding back across the pebbled beach to their home in the sea. Sharp crescent moon bright against blackness, so bright the stars are faint. Moonlight catches the crest of each gentle wave, mesmerizing me with rhythm of light and sound and movement. One would think that after a long day of chores and whatnot, sleep would come more easily. But now that I am aging—I must be nearly forty years by now—sleep is elusive. The effort to stay alive and fed is easier in some ways without a husband to care for, but it's also lonely. I need less. I spend more time than most in the woods and am familiar with what and where to forage. No one knows this, but I follow the local Indians around and watch where they go and what they pick. I am certain they know I am there while not seeming to mind my presence.

I have learned much from them by watching. Disapproval would be swift and harsh if anyone from Marblehead were to catch me. Not that I care for their approval, but they have ways of making life difficult. I cannot comprehend their ways even though I am one of them. The stinking, drab clothing suffocates me. The laws of the church feel like iron bars.

I have my ways of rebelling; my dresses are full of pockets in the seams. I sneak bits of silk and lace into the sleeves and hems. I do not think anyone else can see them, but the small bits of color and texture raise my spirits. Somehow, the town council has convinced all the women to keep watch on one another. If women do their work for them, I suppose this makes their task easier. Rebecca is always watching me, so I go out of my way to give her something to see. Sometimes I sit right in front of her in church to make it easy for her. I am uncertain what her fascination with me is considering we have known each other since both of our families made their way here from Scotland long ago. My baby, Anthony, died, the same year Rebecca's Rae Ann did, and we grieved together. Lots of people died that hungry winter. It was after that I began wandering alone.

At first, I only wanted solitude. The trees and water seemed to absorb my grief. After a time, I began to see the plants and the stones and the Indians moving silently. I began sewing pockets into my dresses to hold the handfuls of things I'd collected and experimenting with concoctions and recipes. Some had dire consequences in the outhouse, but many have become staples in my kitchen.

I cannot allow anyone from Marblehead into my cottage or they will see and draw conclusions. I realize this makes me unsociable, but I can't abide the nosiness and piety of the villagers. I cannot live without them, as I do need supplies on occasion, and do not desire complete isolation. Although, at times complete isolation has its allure.

Before my husband disappeared, he made amends for my rude tongue and procured what we needed from town. Now that he is gone, I am left to navigate on my own and I fear that my reputation may hinder my survival. Cold has seeped through my clothing and into my bones. I rise on aching knees, numbness in my hands and feet, and make my way through the dark to my cottage to the comfort of my bed and the warmth of my cat.

Rebecca

I cannot believe Delfa is wearing ribbons after Reverend Leon specifically railed last Sunday on the evils of finery. I can see blue bows shining right at her elbow in plain sight. She is always showing off, calling attention to herself instead of God. I hope she gets chastised and fined. Her arm twitches in church, and there is a slash in her sleeve with an inset of blue silk peeping out. Next, she will be wearing lace. How can she afford that fabric? She must be living hand to mouth more so than the rest of us, ever since her husband never came home from King Philip's War. She better hope the Wabanaki do not have him. He'd be better off dead. Nobody around here is going to take her in. Everyone hates Delfa for putting on airs. That blue silk is pretty, though, especially with her red hair.

Sarah nudges me sharp in the ribs with her great knob of an elbow, rolling my shoulder blades against the pew back. "Rebecca, somebody sighted a sail. There's a ketch coming into the harbor," she whispers into my ear.

I look up and see bonnets leaning toward each other across the chapel, a soft hiss wisping through the congregation. I fold my cracked fingers into my palms. Lord, let it be Sam. My husband, Sam, has been out there fishing for weeks. We heard the Wabanaki were boarding ketches and murdering crews, one by one. The Wabanaki have guns now, because some arseworm idiots in Salem believed they were telling the truth about the peace treaty. Folks in Salem say the war is over, but they are not living in fear of having their throats cut in their sleep. Or being tossed into the sea to drown. We're still losing our men as if the war didn't take a hefty portion of them already. I haven't any mind to declare peace to a bunch of filthy devils who won't scoot over and make room after God Almighty himself brought us to this empty land. I know they were here first, but we're here now, God's chosen people. I don't know if they can even be saved, as they are more animal than human. Our Lord Jesus Christ brought us here and gave this land to us. It's ours now.

Anyhow, Reverend Leon seems to realize he is losing his audience and is finally wrapping up the service with one more drone of a prayer. As soon as he lets out one last windy Ahhhhhmeeeeennnnnn and blessed be, everybody in the place is on their feet and moving toward the door.

Outside in the street, the shadow of the church still carries a chill as we all huddle together to hear who saw what at the harbor. Delfa edges around the outside of the circle chewing her lip, but don't nobody move over to let her in. Hmpf. Let her eavesdrop. At least half a dozen people are taking credit for spotting the sail, but they were all inside the church, and it doesn't matter anyway.

We all scurry down the road like getting there first is going to make the ketch arrive faster. The huddle moves toward the harbor as one, running now. My heart pounds in my chest; my boots slip in the mud. Sweat breaks out on my neck and wets my armpits. I can hardly breathe and my bladder complains. Sarah's great elbow knob bangs into my shoulder as she gallops beside me and

somebody behind me keeps stepping on my skirt. I throw an elbow of my own backward and make contact with what I can only
assume is a face. I hear a smack and an oof! as I pick up my skirts
in my fists and press forward. That's what they get for crowding.
The congregation is spreading out a little bit now with the
young'uns at the head of the pack and the elders tottering behind.

Mud under my feet turns to pebbles as we near the harbor and
the ever-present stink of dried fish fills my gasping lungs as I slip
to a stop, the wooden heels of my boots losing contest with the
smooth stones of the shore. The precious few men still left in
town congregate on the dock, vying for the right to be correct
about the identity of the ketch in the distance. As if any one of
them can see that far. I shove Sarah aside and squint at the horizon. The sun is full up now and casting glimmers on the water. I
shade my eyes with my hand and stare, willing sails to differentiate
themselves from whitecaps. And then, I see them.

"There! I see it!" I scream, pointing toward the bobbing white
triangle.

I fall to my knees, my hands gripping together as empty sobs
quake my body.

*God Lord in Heaven, let them be alive, let it be Sam, please Jesus God
the Father, please.*

We've been hearing day after day that ketch after ketch has
been taken over, but we don't know if the Wabanaki are killing all
the crews. The last report from up by Salem Neck said a fisher-
man was chucked overboard to drown but managed to find a
piece of wood floating in the bay, and he used it to kick himself
to shore, half-dead by the time he got there. He said those filthy
savages were stripping the fishermen bare and chucking them
over the side if they refused to sail the boat for them. Apparently,
the savages can shoot a gun, but cannot sail a fishing boat. And a

week past, an empty ketch beached down south a-ways. No one left on board, just blood on the deck.

I kneel in the stones and sand surrounded by muddy skirts and chattering voices, the damp seeping through my cotton petticoats. Hope and rage choking my breath. I cannot see the boat approaching from the ground, so I hobble to my feet, grasping Sarah's dangling arm with a grip like death. Her boys were out there with my husband, Sam. She is just as scared as me, even though her face does not show it. We know it will be awhile before the boat gets to us, but we can see now it is coming straight for the harbor.

We wait.

Every woman on the beach has lost a son, a brother, a husband, or all three, and as the afternoon sun shifts our shadows, we pass around our stories of loss and sorrow, blame and fear, like poison tea. Delfa stays back from the group, her full lips set grim and tight. I know she is still hoping for her husband's return, but no one cares. It's her own fault for being uppity and mean. Her husband is not out there on a fishing boat, anyway. He never came back from the war. Just disappeared.

We wait.

As the sun begins to slide back toward town, the ketch lurches suddenly into plain view. Captain Robert Roules, a Marblehead man, is on deck, hollering and waving and throwing rope, wearing nothing but a bloody shirt and tattered drawers. Two other fishermen struggle alongside Robert. They were from Captain Watt's ketch, which I know because that's who all of our men set out with. So if our men aren't here, they must be dead.

I see no sign of Sam.

Then I see the Wabanaki. Captain Roules and his men haul two bound-up Indians to the plank.

We all start screaming when we see those Wabanaki with their arms tied behind their backs and their mouths bound shut. Roules and the others push them onto the dock, high stepping them toward the beach. Their eyes go wide at the sight of us waiting for them.

"Hand 'em over!" Sarah yells.

Us women echo her call.

Roules steps down from the pier in front of us with his ragged drawers hanging down underneath his shirtwaist. "Hey now, ladies, clear a path. We're taking these Indians to the constable. Just everybody calm down."

Sarah steps forward and me, right behind her. "I'll be damned if you are going to give them murderers a trial and set 'em free. Hand 'em over," Sarah yells.

Rocks sail from the crowd and near-miss Roules's head. He ducks. "Ladies, ladies, we are going to let the law decide. Step aside—"

Sarah punches Roules in the face, which has to hurt because her knuckles are as knobby as her elbows and she has a reach like a man. Roules stumbles back and I step in to shove him to the ground. He falls and loses his grip on the prisoner.

As the prisoner lurches to find his balance, I lunge for his throat. The howl I give doesn't sound like me. As my hands close in, I feel the soft flesh of his brown throat move across what lies beneath his skin. I push my weight onto him and he falls, his head colliding onto stones and water. I sink my fingernails into the softness below his ears and pull. His face is so close to mine I can smell the musk of his skin. The crush of women feels hot around my body and their roar fills my head. I glance up to see Sarah grab the other prisoner by the hair and proceed to raise his head and beat it back down onto the rocks, blood spurting from his nose.

Women surround me, pulling at the Indians' hair and skin. At this point, I am sitting on top of this murderer with no mind to my skirts hiked above my knees, fingers digging deeper into his throat. His eyes roll back in his head. He is still breathing. I can hear it from the gurgles in his throat. My hand closes around a palm-sized stone, and I raise it over my head. My fingers, numb with cold, can't feel my grip as I bring the stone down onto his temple. Again and again. The howls of the women around me seem far away. Again and again.

"Come on, now. Come on, Rebecca," Sarah's voice cuts through. "Get off! He's dead."

I come into myself as Sarah's man-hands haul me up onto my feet and I see what I've done. My throat is raw from screaming. *How did this happen?* I wonder.

I hang onto Sarah's warmth, my throat dry as a bone and my breath coming in shudders. My skirts, dripping with seawater and blood, cling to my legs. I look at my hands as Sarah peels my fingers from the stone they still clutch, which drops to the sand. My fingernails are caked with blood and skin. Sarah leads me, wobbling, to the water.

"Here now, rinse your hands, splash your face. We did it, sister. It's done," Sarah says in a voice calm as prayer.

I dip my hands into the sea and stretch out my fingers. I cannot feel them.

"Here now, rub them together like so." Sarah takes my hands and rubs them together for me, closing her big, knobby mitts around mine, and together we rinse the Indians' blood from between our fingers. I watch the cloud of red disperse into the lapping waves.

"Rinse your face, Rebecca," she says.

I cup the sea and hunch forward to meet my palms, the smell of it all coming into focus, blood and fish and wet wool. The water in my hands turns red from the blood that must be all over my face.

"Come on now. Let's go home," Sarah says, and I follow her. As we turn back to the beach, I can see the crowd dispersing, leaving the bodies of the Wabanaki in pieces on the shore.

"Take that to the constable," I say to Sarah with a laugh that comes out as a shaking croak, and chills set into my limbs.

"Only God's judgment awaits them now." Sarah smiles.

As we pass the bodies, I reach down and pick up a scrap of leather that lies in the sand. We trudge on toward my house, where Sarah comes in to sit with me.

Sam has not returned. Nor Sarah's boys. Maybe they still will, but if not, at least they are avenged. We make a fire and tea and have a nipperkin, too, if I'm honest. We strip off our dresses in front of the flames, shivering and cold to the bone. Wrapped up in quilts, Sarah regales me of happenings at the shore which I do not remember. She has an uncanny recollection of who used what to abuse who. Her boys are not coming back, and those Indians got what they deserved, she says.

"Sam is not coming back, either, you know," she says, curling up in her chair—no easy feat with her lanky legs hanging off the side—and she nods off.

I pull my three-legged stool right up to the hearth and as I inspect my hands, I let the heat of the flames sear my skin. The worn cracks in my tired fingers are etched red with bloodstain. I use one broken fingernail to carve out what lies beneath another: bits of brown skin.

Sarah snorts softly in her sleep. I pull the bit of leather out of my apron pocket and smooth it out over my leg, tracing the design carved into the band and drawing the salt-stiffened hide between my fingers. I think about what Sarah said regarding Sam not coming back.

So be it.

Sarah startles awake before sunrise, sitting straight up in bed beside me, which is where we ended up last night after the fire died. "I best get home," she groans and slides out from underneath the quilt.

I burrow in deeper as she hikes up her shift and squats over my chamber pot in the corner, her stream splashing against the side.

"Just leave it. I'll toss it later," I mumble from under the quilt.

"All right, then, thank-ee." Sarah swabs herself with her shift and pulls her dress on over her head.

"Need a hand?" I ask, hoping she does not.

"Nope, don't get up," Sarah grunts, reaching her fingers between her shoulder blades, flicking buttons into loops. She slips out the door into still darkness.

As I roll over, my bladder lurches. I crawl out from under the covers, bare feet on packed earth, flip my shift up around my waist and squat, adding to Sarah's puddle. *At least she didn't shite.* I return to bed, something I have never done before. Sam is not coming back. I pull the quilt up to my chin, fingering the loose stitches on the corner. The day stretches out ahead. Weed the garden. Peas need picking. I have been helping Sarah with her livestock in return for milk and eggs. Lord knows there isn't much else to eat. *Sam is not coming back.*

I lie in bed looking at my Sunday dress hanging by the fireplace, dried stiff with salt water. I'll never get the blood out. I groan in the dark, my body aching. *What would happen if I stayed right here? Starve to death, that's what. And I'd go to Hell for sloth too.*

Get up, woman, I order myself. *This is the day the Lord hath made.* I straighten the bedclothes and pull on my everyday dress and apron and tighten my bonnet over my twisted bun, tucking loose strands behind my ears. I pick up the still-warm chamber pot, acrid tang wafting up my nose. As I hoist it into the crook of my arm, a wave of urine sloshes onto my apron, the pot being fuller than usual. I reckon it's laundry day, as well.

I fling the pot's remaining contents into the weeds at the back of the garden, careful to miss the small mound and wooden cross where my baby Rae Ann is laid to rest. So long ago now. Fifteen years gone by since that winter that would not quit. We all about starved to death and my milk dried up. I had nothing for her. She passed away in her papa's arms. Sam was never the same after that.

Pink scraping across the sky, I stand in the yard breathing the quiet. Remembering the feel of Rae Ann's little body, nothing but skin and bones, laid weightless in the earth. Dirt between my toes, empty house, surrounded, but alone. How is it just me now? The long trip here as a child, only to have every last person taken away. Scripture interrupts my thoughts like a reflex, saving my soul from despair.

We glory in tribulations also: knowing that tribulation worketh patience.

How patient do I have to be? *Lord, don't strike me down for my evil thoughts.* Quiet is haunting my mind. Sam will never walk back through that door. My heart knows he is dead. I recite another verse under my breath as birds wake and someone's rooster crows.

Yea doubtless, and I count all things but loss for the excellency of the knowledge of Christ Jesus my Lord: for whom I have suffered the loss of all things, and do count them but dung, that I may win Christ.

I grab a handful of peas off the vine and shove one in my mouth. The pod snaps between my teeth and I rip off the stem and toss it in the dirt. Again and again, suddenly ravenous, I eat my way through the peas like the glutton I am and then start in on the greens, wrenching off whole handfuls of lettuce and stuffing them in my gullet. There won't be anything left if I keep at it. Instead, I grab the splintered hoe handle and attack weeds like a mad woman. By the time I am done, the sun is high in the sky and I'm sour with sweat.

I gather up my blood-soaked Sunday dress, urine-soaked apron, and the clouts from my last course in the wooden tub, throw in a cake of soap, and head out to the creek. Some folks haul water to the yard for laundry, but that makes for a backache. Easier to lug the bucket downstream and hope for no company. It is not safe outside the town gate, but I am going anyway. As I walk the path to where Forest River flows over the rocks into Massachusetts Bay, I pray.

Be sober, be vigilant; because your adversary the Devil, as a roaring lion, walketh about, seeking whom he may devour.

With every step, I repeat the words that will keep the Devil out of my head and the Indians away from my washing spot.

Forest River spreads before me, water rushing over boulders at the entrance to the bay. After turning my clothing onto the ground, I clamber to the water's edge and lower my bucket into the foaming swirls between the rocks. The tub fills and I throw my soiled clouts in to soak. I raise and lower my Sunday dress into the river, hands instantly numb, gripping tightly against the current, raising and lowering until the fabric soaks through, rinsing out the salt and grit from the day before. I use smooth stones to pound last year's lye soap into the bloodstains, but they won't budge. I give up too fast, spread my dress out on the riverbank to dry, and reach back into the bucket where my clouts soak at the bottom. I swirl them around, loosening the rehydrated rivulets of my own rusted flowers, which do not come so often anymore. They dissolve in a red cloud, filling the frigid water in the bucket. I pound my stained clouts, the rhythm of the rock against the boulders in the stream bringing visions of the Indian's face, flesh ripping away from bone as the suds flood my hands. Again and again.

When the clouts are as clean as they can be, I spread them out to dry in the sun and think about dinner. I have no meat and do not want to ask for charity. One cannot borrow a chicken. There might be lobster down the beach. It will be stinking in this heat, but maybe I can find some that have not been dead overlong.

I walk down the shoreline, sun baking the top of my head, scanning for beached lobster. I come across a couple of shells in the low tide and give one a nudge with my toe. A swarm of flies rises and settles. *I am not that hungry.* Something moves in the water, a shadow in the wake. A seal? That might mean fish are around. The shadow flashes again, closer to the surface and white this time. I freeze as something unholy rises straight up out of the wave. That is not a seal. *Oh Lord have mercy, what is it?* Is it an angel? A demon? A witch? What kind of creature rises up out of the deep on two legs?

The figure in the water gleams white in the unbroken sun, seawater flowing from streaming hair and naked skin. I hold my breath and blink to make the apparition go away. *Be sober, be vigilant* . . . Still there. It is some kind of supernatural she-devil. She falters, finds footing on the graveled sand, bracing against the tide as she wraps her long hair in her hands, wringing it out. She twists her wet mane around itself, lays it across her shoulder, and approaches the beach with careful steps, some strange object hanging from a string around her neck.

I fall to my knees, hands clasped, and repeat the Lord's Prayer as fast as I can with my eyes squinched shut. *Is she coming for me?* I open my eyes expecting to see her sprout wings and fly toward me on a flaming cross or some damn thing.

Wait.

No.

That's Delfa.

Delfa reaches the sand and her pile of abandoned clothing. She does not see me, or pretends not to, and lies right down in the sand, prone like a harlot. I have never seen a naked body before, not even my own, except for little Rae Ann when she was a baby.

God Almighty, we are not supposed to be naked in between the womb and the grave. I am never without a shift on. Not even my own husband ever saw me without a shift. I never even seen my whole self without it. "Naked came I out of my mother's womb, and naked shall I return thither: the Lord gave, and the Lord hath taken away; blessed be the name of the Lord," I chant, rocking back and forth.

Delfa, or the demon in her, seems to be sleeping in the sun, her soft down glinting red as it dries. Pale breasts slack, red-brown nipples softening on her chest, the amulet rising and falling with her breath. *She's the one sinning, but seeing her is a sin too, and she forced this vision onto my eyes through no fault of my own. I heard it whispered she's a witch and now I can see that it is true.* But I sit and stare and wonder how do I get out of here. She can't know I seen her. This is every kind of trouble.

Jesus.

Delfa's eyes are still closed, so I pick myself up and ease away. When I get out of eyesight, I take off in a run until I get to my washing, gather everything up, and shove it all, still damp, into the bucket, scrambling for the slippery bar of lye soap. I run pell-mell back to the town gate, bucket banging my leg.

Our Father, which art in Heaven, Hallowed be Thy name.
Thy Kingdom come.
Feet pound the path.
Thy will be done on earth,
As it is in Heaven.
Heart bursting.
Give us this day our daily bread.
Gasping side-stitch.
And forgive us our trespasses,
As we forgive them that trespass against us.
Washtub strains my shoulder.
And lead us not into temptation,
I did not mean to look.
But deliver us from evil.
Slam the door open and shut, plunk the bucket down on the floor.
For Thine is the Kingdom,
The power, and the glory,
For ever and ever.
Amen.

My hands shake as I light too many pitch pine knots and the fire bellows to life. No time for mildew. I hang my dress and apron to dry, willing my heart to steady. String my clouts and shifts out on the table. No need to hide them away with Sam gone. A rap at the door and I startle. Sarah bursts in.

"What is it? Why're you running? You're dead-white, Rebecca."

"I am scared to tell you what I saw, Sarah. I do not know if it was real or not. Maybe I imagined it, maybe it was a vision sent from the Devil to test me."

"Out with it, woman."

I tell Sarah what I saw. It is unspeakable, but I find words.

Sarah's eyes widen. "Only a witch would do such a thing. Did you pray? Ask for forgiveness for witnessing such abomination."

"I did, I did, I did, I prayed all the way home. I did not look on purpose."

That's a lie. Forgive me, Lord Jesus, for lying. Forgive me for looking. I am sinking.

"Well. Reverend Leon would say you must have sin in your heart or the Devil would not be able to play tricks on you. Something to think about. Come have dinner with me and settle yourself down. You can repent later."

My stomach growls a response. Those peas I ate this morning are long gone. I follow Sarah home. Over beans and cornbread, Sarah and me contemplate Delfa's disregard for godly modesty and possible possession by the Devil himself as proved by her tendency toward self-decoration and vanity. Never mind the sickness that comes from bathing. Everybody knows getting water all over your skin will be your death, no matter what the Wabanaki say. They take off their garments and rub water on their skin with no modesty whatsoever. Constantly chewing on herbs and rubbing sticks on the teeth. It is a wonder such activities do not kill them, but there's all the proof you need that they aren't the same as us. So long as your shifts are clean, you're clean. It is the undergarments that get dirty. Delfa should know better, as scripture applies to her as a child of God. She has the whitest skin I have ever seen.

"Delfa is alone now too, you know," Sarah says. "Rumor is she's going on the poor fund."

"What? She spent precious coin on that blue silk, and now the town has to take care of her? That is not right. I have nothing to spare. I am two steps away from the vendue myself."

"Ha! She spent all that on a new dress and still won't wear clothes." Sarah guffaws, showing her back teeth.

"It isn't funny, Sarah. The Devil's got ahold of her and she is going to bring the wrath of the Lord down on us all."

Sarah stops laughing. "Maybe so. I was going to trade her some eggs for her silk scraps, but her wares are probably cursed. Anyway, you do not have to donate to the poor fund; it's the landowning men that support vendue—and Sam is gone. One of them will take Delfa for hire until she is too old and then she will go to the poorhouse. It is better than starving, you know."

I wander home in the dusk, belly full for once. The night shadows hoot as stars emerge, half-moon following through a break in the clouds. Shivers skitter my skin as I pull my door closed and slip into bed quick. Silence smothers me as the permanent emptiness of the house settles around. I drift off to sleep.

She comes to me in a dream. Walking on water in the night, right over the tops of the silver break line. Floating naked toward me, moonlight illuminates her hair like a burnished halo. Gleaming off her white shoulders, her face in shadow. Steady rhythm of waves slap the shore. Her arms above her head as she rises into the air and swaths me like smoke, suddenly here. My shift, gone. Honeysuckle breath on my face and her pink lips turn blood-red against my collarbone, her amulet of twigs and twine lacing my stomach. The full weight of her settles onto my hips, my nipples tighten and rise as her breasts brush mine. My knees slide up her thighs, my fingers catch in her snarled curls. I can't look away from Delfa's green eyes, right up until the moment our lips touch and her tongue, hot as fire, licks mine.

I jolt awake, sitting upright. I cannot breathe. Demon spirit choking me. Tongue scorched, collarbone burning. I run my hands over the patchwork quilt. *She is gone. She is not here.*

But I say unto you,
I lie back,
That whosoever looketh on a woman
pulse pounds my ears,
to lust after her
breath coming shallow,
hath committed adultery with her already in his heart.
I lift my shift beneath the quilt.

Rebecca

Names are being floated around, who is pairing up with whom now that so many of our men are dead and gone. The younger girls can have their pick of husbands from here to Boston. However, any upright man would solve a lot of problems for me. I'm about past childbearing, and so is Sarah, which has its advantages. I can keep a house and garden and not have to worry about babies, even raise somebody else's if I have to. Sarah's brother-in-law is obliged to provide for her, but I am alone and my options are limited. Reverend Leon holds my gaze lately, longer than he should. I have noticed.

I am on my way to the meeting house this holy Sunday morning and I intend to ask for special prayer from Reverend Leon. The Devil keeps visiting my dreams in the form of Delfa and I am afraid he is trying to steal my soul. After every dream, I wake to a red cross on my stomach where Delfa's amulet brushed my skin. Witchery is everywhere nowadays; everybody knows that, and I feel I need some special attention from the Lord. While I am at it, perhaps I can gain further attention from Reverend Leon too. To that end I have remade my Sunday dress so as to remove the reminder of that bloody day on the beach.

I sleep with my Bible on my chest every night now, and never neglect my prayers, but still the dreams come. It has gotten so I am afraid to go to sleep. If I should die before I wake and the Devil has visited a dream upon me in the night, I might go straight to Hell without ever waking up. I cannot bear this burden.

My spine smacks into the pew as I sit down, knocking a tingle up my backbone. I squint at Reverend Leon standing behind the pulpit. Someone is keeping him fed. From the way his waistcoat buttons strain over his belly and his collars are white as can be, he obviously has enough to share. Rumor has it Delfa has been lurking around the boarding house, trying to catch his attention or worse, but now that the town has hired him as our permanent minister, he is setting up at the parsonage. She will not be sneaking in the back door there, or we will hear of it.

Speaking of, Delfa sways in late like she owns the place and sits on the pew in front of me, which is not right. When her husband was around, he held no place on the council. Her assigned seat is in the back, but that is just like her to presume a position regardless. Her hair is not even tucked into her bonnet, and that sinful blue silk is looking tattered as a whore's twat. When Delfa bows her head for prayer, a tendril of red curl slips down the back of her neck and I press my knees together. I have to look away. I know the Devil must be possessing her to give me these thoughts, and she would let him too, for spite.

Rumor has it her husband is not dead; he just did not want to come home. Because of Delfa's sharp tongue, most likely. Last Sunday, the town council tried to put her on the poor fund and she turned it down like she had a choice in the matter. If she does not agree to it, they will auction her off for vendue—as if anybody would bid on her. She thinks she can support herself selling potions, penny loaves, and wilted cabbages. Maybe when I'm

married to Reverend Leon she can come clean the parsonage for
me. I rub my apron over my mouth to hide a snicker. I best be
cautious, though, or I will end up on the poor fund myself, a
thought that wipes my smile away.

I turn my eyes to Reverend Leon. If I look long and hard
enough, I can imagine snuggling up to that bear of a man. Keep
me warm, anyway. He is a hellfire preacher, though, and I wonder
if he relaxes at home or if the smoke from the woodstove makes
him nervous. He could back the Devil down out of the fireplace
with that deep, gravelly voice of his. At the moment, his prayer
seems like it is going to be as long as the sermon that is sure to
follow. I watch his neck waggle and spit burble in the corners of
his thick lips. A spot of stray whiskers wobbles on his chin and as
his arms wave around, sweat beads up on his temples. I close my
eyes to shut out the sight and concentrate on his voice. I think if
I keep my eyes closed, it will be all right.

"Praise be to our Lord and Savior Jesus Christ. Let all ye who
enter here be pure of body, mind, and soul . . . We come before
you as humble servants, Almighty God . . ."

His timbre resonates through the pew, and I can feel the vibrations all kinds of places, and when he shouts, "Mercy upon us,
Lord!" I jump and shoot my eyes open.

Reverend Leon carries on about Eve and the apple and how
she brought sin down on us all. He sure does like that story.

"And the Lord God said unto the woman,

What is this that thou hast done?

And the woman said,

The serpent beguiled me, and I did eat."

And I notice that Delfa's red curl is untucked again and hanging down the back of her neck like a little snake. And then he
keeps going, talking about how Eve tempted Adam and blamed

it on the snake, but really it's her fault and she got the entirety of humanity banished from the Garden of Eden, all because she could not resist a little temptation. And I cannot breathe remembering Delfa on the beach, and the pew beneath me rocks like a boat on the waves, and I don't know why I am thinking about all that in the middle of church. Surely, God can see my thoughts.

Reverend Leon has switched topics and somehow he is on about the lusts of the flesh, like he can read my mind. He has jumped from Genesis all the way to Matthew and this service will never end. My tailbone is about to break. I look away from Delfa's stupid neck and see Reverend Leon looking right at me, quoting Matthew 5:28 like he means it for me: "But I say unto you, that whosoever looketh on a woman to lust after her hath committed adultery with her already in his heart."

I feel like he can see right through me and my knees shiver. I hold his gaze to show I am not sinning and am in full agreement, but his black eyes burn right into me. Pinpricks start in my armpits. The pew is still quaking under me like a storm brewing in the sea. Reverend Leon's lips are moving, but I cannot hear his words. Delfa's whispers in the night seem to be coming out of Reverend Leon's mouth, interspersed with the hiss of a snake. Chills fill me and my face flushes hot. My left leg shoots straight out, knocking my ankle into the pew in front of me, and pain rockets to my hip. Delfa jolts upright and turns to glare, her lips saying *what?* like she does not know what is going on.

Reverend Leon keeps going, never looking away from me. Scripture falls like poetry from his lips.

"For the lips of an adulteress drip honey
And smoother than oil is her speech;
But in the end she is bitter as wormwood,
Sharp as a two-edged sword.

Her feet go down to death,

Her steps take hold of Sheol."

Needles seem to jab between my fingers and I feel the most wrenching pain as they curl backward in my lap of their own accord, as though the Devil himself is pulling them back to my wrist bones. Blood seeps out the cracks around my fingernails, running onto my apron. Breath coming shallow, my back arches, pulling me up out of my seat, and I screech.

"It is her," I say, pointing at Delfa. "Witch, witch, witch!" I call out.

I scream and sob, "Witch, witch, witch."

Needles all over my back and such a jerking in my belly I cannot control. My chest convulses—huh, huh, huh—but cannot catch breath. The air has gone dim.

Reverend Leon strides down from the pulpit, a dark angel, robes billowing, and catches me as I fall. "I call upon the name of the Lord Jesus to protect our Sister Rebecca from Satan himself," he thunders.

The town councilmen jump out of the pews and haul Delfa to the front of the church, forcing her to her knees. Holding her there.

Delfa looks confused and says to me, she yells, "What is wrong with you, you crazy cunt?" and everybody gasps at her foul mouth.

Reverend Leon holds my arms down with those bear paws and their warmth calms my shaking soul. I feel a softness come over my heart as he lowers me back down to my pew and solemnly lumbers to the front of the church, his head bowed.

"Art thou a witch, woman?" he asks Delfa, towering over her.

"No," Delfa snaps, still on the floor, looking scared now.

The judge stands from his seat in the front row and orders the town councilmen to haul Delfa down to the courthouse. They jostle to grab ahold of Delfa's arms, yanking her this way and that as she trips over her hem.

"Rebecca, tell them it's not true." She looks at me wild-eyed, but I look away, rocking back and forth on the pew. Clasp my hands to my breast and bow my head. My heart thuds behind my hands.

"Say no more, Delfa," the judge orders. "At the very least you stand charged with wearing excess apparel."

"What in fuck," she mutters as they drag her out the door.

The congregation disperses in uneasy silence and Reverend Leon cordially invites me to the parsonage for tea and comfort after service. He gathers my hands between his thick palms and prays out loud, right at his kitchen table, and the Spirit of the Lord descends into the room. He says the demons are gone and I should rest in the comfort of the Lord. Then he tucks his fingers under my chin, grasps it gently, and asks for my hand in marriage—as I surely need protecting. The parsonage has three rooms and glass windows. I accept his offer.

I wonder what's happening to Delfa in jail while she awaits trial. I speculate maybe she wants to repent, but Reverend Leon says I ought not go see her, because the Devil knows the pathways of my mind and it is not safe for someone so spiritually delicate as me. He reminds me that the Bible says, "Thou shalt not suffer a witch to live." Her fate is in the Lord's hands now and we best leave it there.

Sarah snuck over to the jail to see, though. She doesn't feel sorry for Delfa, of course, but she is curious about her situation. Sarah can't ever resist knowing things. Sarah said she had to climb a tree to get a good look through the iron bars of the jail cell. She said the stench of an unemptied chamber pot reached all the way to the outside and she could see Delfa huddled in the corner covered in red blisters. Anyway, Sarah said it may be what Delfa deserves, but I think no soul should suffer in that rat-infested pit. Living like that, covered in lice and with just one threadbare blanket, it is a wonder she is not already dead. Hanging will be a mercy after that.

Rumor has it Delfa cannot wait for trial at home until she can pay her excess-wear fine, and room and board at the jail racks up faster than anybody could ever pay it. The price of her chains alone would bankrupt most, which is just as well, because those iron bars must be keeping her spirit in. I have not had any more dreams since she was locked up and I married Reverend Leon.

Delfa stands on the gallows, thin as a rail, still in her church dress after all this time, sagging in places where curves once swelled. Those blue-silk slashed sleeves were ripped out by the seams and her filthy elbows poke out the holes. Greasy red curls now limp on her shoulders. Vacant eyes drift over the crowd. I shove my way forward and her weary eyes settle on me. I feel no pangs, no pull toward her. Seems even the Devil has abandoned her and left her powerless. She keeps her gaze on me as a rope, thick as a fist, lowers around her neck and tightens, pulling at the white skin of her throat. My neck prickles and itches, as if the coarse fibers of the rope are digging into my own neck and the weight of the noose compressing my shoulders. The tang of unwash and fresh sweat fills my nose as the murmur of the crowd swells, punctuated by shouts of "Witch!"

The harrumphing judge announces Delfa, sentenced to hang this day for the crime of witchcraft. Leon stands alongside—

strangely dis-familiar to me in this moment—and drones a prayer, then quotes Leviticus:

"A man also or woman that hath a familiar spirit, or that is a wizard, shall surely be put to death: they shall stone them with stones: their blood shall be upon them."

Leon and the judge step aside and the executioner grasps the rope in gloved hands. I feel the crowd growing louder all around me, but I cannot hear them. My stomach clenches as the rope tugs under my chin. Delfa's green eyes, bright as emerald now, bear into mine with a strange light and my heart races as the rope tightens, pricking fibers like tiny knives in my throat. Breath snorts into my lungs as my throat fights constriction. The only sound is the executioner's grunt as he heaves the rope. My airways are cut off as my body swings upward, then down. I want to gag but cannot. Shakes convulse me as the day turns black and my body goes limp. Light blasts my closed eyelids. I open my eyes to see Delfa's strangled, lifeless body swinging in the noose, surprised to still be standing among the pressing crowd. Tremors subside as my burning lungs fill with chilled autumn air. I unclench my fists to see that my fingernails have incised deep punctures that I cannot feel into my palms. The sunlight leaves me lightheaded.

"God Almighty, I am glad that's over," Sarah declares as she grabs me by the arm, turning back toward town, shopping basket banging her hip. "You're safe now, sis." She gives my shoulders a little shake. "Come on, now. Are you all right?"

"I'm fine. Just need a cup of tea," I whisper into her sleeve.

Sarah marches me to the parsonage and puts the kettle on for me. I watch her navigate my kitchen like it is her own, grateful for her bustling good nature as she hands me a steaming mug.

"You ever wonder why she let the Devil do it, Sarah?" I ask. "Do you think she knew the Devil was working through her? Did you ever wonder if she realized what the Devil was using her for and did she go along with it, or was she just a vessel? When she visited me with evil dreams, was she really there or did the Devil just use her image?"

"Oh Lord have mercy, Rebecca. Who knows? What difference does it make? Delfa was always more bitch than witch, anyway. It's good she's gone."

Leon comes in as Sarah goes out, wraps me up in his great bear hug, and pulls me onto the narrow ledge of his lap. I lean into him, kiss his scrubbled cheek, and bury my face into the fold of his neck. I stay there a long while.

Story Five:
Tarbert 1567

Delfa

Magistrate steps toward me, fist white-knuckled around the iron
cage of the scold's bridle; his thin lips sneer and sharp nostrils
twitch as he smells my fear. I close my eyes. Darkness fills me,
spangles of light float wildly against my eyelids, the wooden heel
of his boot clacks against the stone courthouse floor. Papery fingers curl around my chin and yank upward. My eyes fly open as
his sour breath engulfs my nose. He grunts softly as he hefts the
cage of curved iron bars over my head; cold iron chain slinks and
coils into my lap. I can feel the bridle in the air, a menace vibrating
above my skull, and glance upward to see it hovering there, iron
hinges hanging loosely. Light gleams on the pointed spikes that
cover the tongue plate, top and bottom.

A moment of silence, a breath. And then, Magistrate lowers
the bridle onto my shoulders, the iron collar collides with my clav-
icles, and iron bars stripe my forehead and temples. The bridle
encases my head. He has taken my cap, and now the iron joint at
the top of the bridle presses into my scalp without mercy. With a
jolt, he yanks the cage back. Rigid bars triangulate around my nose
as the spiked tongue plate slices between my lips, cleaving my
tongue. Hot gush of blood fills my mouth as the plate cuts into

the back of my throat, sharp spikes rake the roof of my mouth and tongue, searing pain as my palate rips open. I gag on blood as he pulls the hinges closed behind my neck and snaps the lock into place, metal screech in my ear. Coughing as the spiked plate jams against the back of my throat and the passage is overcome with a pool of blood. As his hands release the cage, my head falls forward and I retch, bloody mucus stringing into my lap atop the links of chain. I judder air into my lungs through my throat, hear it whistle inside my head as it forces its way around the spikes. A sob escapes me, my throat convulsing around the plate, and I retch again.

"Calm yourself," Magistrate barks. "Punishment as fits the crime."

I take another shaking gasp and force breath out of my nostrils. Everything burns. I inhale through my nose and will my throat to relax around the spikes forcing their way into the ripped roof of my mouth.

"On your feet, Delfa."

He retrieves the chain lead from my lap with two prim fingers and slips the ring onto a hook anchored in the mortar of the hearth. Pulls me forward. I stumble on the brick lip of the hearth and catch myself on the wall, the sudden jolt pushing the bar farther into my throat, choking me. My lips crack and spread around the bar, stinging with the salt of my inadvertent tears. As I reach for the chain, the thud of his cane handle cracks the back of my hand, its jeweled crest splitting the thin skin stretched across my knuckles.

"Do not think to free yourself," he snarls and grabs my apron strings with his left hand, lifting me to my bare toes. With his right, he nudges my hip with his cane handle, burrowing the knob into my buttock. He pushes me forward, then leans in close, his lips practically brushing the iron bars, his breath hot and fetid on the back of my neck. Shaking, I plant my palms on the hearth bricks below the hook where I am attached.

Magistrate drops his hands and hoists my skirt and shift up my back, sticks his cane between my knees, whacking back and forth. I step my feet apart, bracing myself against the bricks. All I can see is the rough red texture of brick between my hands, the iron bar a blurred shadow between my eyes. He fumbles with his clothing, and then comes hot, searing pain. Every thrust bumps the cage into the bricks and shoves the spiked tongue plate of the bridle deeper into my throat. I cannot scream, only choke and gag on the metal. He finishes quickly with a grunt, drops my skirts, retrieves his dropped cane from the floor.

Magistrate shrugs on his overcoat and adjusts his hat. I stand with quivering knees as he unhooks the ring from the hook and moves toward the door. I have no choice but to follow. He steps down onto the street as I stumble behind. I can barely see around the iron bar that bridges my nose and cheeks, and I trip on the step. He gives the chain a quick yank.

"Come now. To the square."

My feet sink into the muddy road. I had no time to retrieve my shoes when Magistrate appeared at my door this morning. He entered my cottage without warning, hauled me outside by the elbow, and marched me to the courthouse without a word. The air went dim like the morning sun had shrunk behind clouds.

Cold slime of mud and dung slips between my toes and with each step I slide. My hands brush against the vomit still clinging to my apron. Magistrate clears his throat, squares his shoulders, and marches a little quicker as we turn toward the town square. My breath comes quick and shallow, hot and moist on the iron cage. As I hold my hands out to balance, something squishy pelts right on top of the cut from Magistrate's cane and a hoot comes from the side of the road.

"Scold!" A peal of laughter rings out.

I cannot turn my head to see who taunts me but hear a gathering of voices. I slide my eyes to the sound. A group of boys gather to jeer. One launches a rock at my head, and it clangs off the bar over my ear, ringing through my skull.

"Shrew!"

"Nag!"

"Hoor!"

The gathering crowd walks alongside us now. Another pelt and squish on my shoulder and the smell of fresh cow dung fills my nose. A sob lurches in my throat and I wonder if Antony is there, and if he will defend me. Please, no. I cannot bear for him to see.

The voices of the crowd swell. The iron collar compresses my throat as I crane my neck to see my feet. Magistrate slows our pace for dramatic effect as crowds form on either side of us. Insults ring through the cold spring air. Rocks submerged in the mud slice my feet. I pull my head up to check the distance to the square, eyes watering as raw tongue shifts under the iron plate, blood and metal. Surely, we must be there by now. And then I see her. Rebecca stands just back from the road, face in shadow beneath her cap. Her narrow shoulders hunch to her ears as I pass, my gaze boring through the air, daring her to meet my eyes.

Little Rae Ann, who I delivered from Rebecca eight years ago, tucks in behind her, big brown eyes staring solemnly at my humiliation. The hem of my skirt dragging in the mud catches under my toe, causing me to stumble. The onlookers cackle as I fall to my knees. The spikes in my mouth puncture farther into my throat and a fresh gush of blood threads out around the iron gag.

"Up, up," Magistrate barks.

I groan with the attempt to right myself but step on the hem of my sodden dress again, the weight of the cage throwing my head off-balance. Magistrate plays to the crowd, huffing and smirking with hands on his hips as I right myself. He rattles the chain and prods me with his cane. The villagers respond with laughter.

Magistrate leads me to the wooden platform and up the steps beside the pillory. He clinks the iron ring at the end of the chain onto a high post hook. I stand before the crowd, all gathered now, and see my son Antony at the back, watching in silent stillness as Magistrate unfurls a parchment. He reads aloud, raising his voice to carry over the gathering.

Delfa Cameron,

You are hereby accused of the following crimes:

Malicious gossip against the Holy Father Leon

What? Who?

Heresy

Rebecca

Lies

All true. She knows it was all true

Taking the Lord's name in vain

Well, yes, but I was deep in ale, as was she

Public drunkenness

Ah-ahhhhh

Promiscuity

They all asked for it, begged even

Witchcraft

I do not understand why herbs and chants fix things, truly I do not. Am I a witch?

"Your punishment is as follows." His pompous voice announces my fate.

Four hours in the bridle on the pillory

Four hours. My legs will collapse beneath me. I will never be able to hold my bladder that long.

Banishment

The crowd whoops.

Surely not. Banishment?

Return on pain of death

I cannot. I cannot. Where will I go? What about Antony?

My heart flutters and flaps wildly like a bird trapped between hands.

Magistrate steps down from the platform to join Father Leon, and they head back toward the courthouse as the crowd gathers to stare and mock. I stand still, as still as I can. Heat rises in my face and my guts churn. I search the crowd for Antony's dark curls, but he has gone. A maggoty potato thumps me in the chest, bouncing off my leather rune pouch that always hangs around my neck. I feel the carved stones collide with my breastbone. The wooden slats of the platform beneath my feet hold me in place against the incoming volley of insults, rotten vegetables, rocks, and dung. Surely, they will tire of this entertainment.

I steady my breath and my heart. Allow the spiked gag to rest on my tongue and against my relaxed throat. *Breathe in. Breathe out.* I watch for Antony but see only Rae Ann's sober gaze. Her brown eyes—so like Antony's—seem to fill her face. Antony and Rae Ann. They have the same steady, all-seeing gaze under luxuriant brows and lashes, the pug nose. The wide, full lips. Just like Father Leon's. *I see it now. How could I have never seen it before?*

I remember when Rae Ann took her first breath and I swaddled her in soft linen from my own spindle, it was like looking at my own child. Antony was a boy then, still clear-faced and soft, not the sullen young man he has become. Little Rae Ann has always had an affinity for me and I for her. She stops by my cottage for herbs and bread and yarn more often than she needs to, more often than Rebecca sends her, and follows Antony around like a little sister. I find her in the yard, stroking the cat in a spot of sunshine, picking blossoms from the garden, rolling herbs between her fingers, smelling their lemony tang. She watches me now in silence from behind her mother's skirts.

I confessed to my indiscretions with Father Leon to Rebecca. Too much ale and a loose tongue encouraged me to gamble secrets for sisterhood. As we sat in the pub, I told her that Leon would visit me in our younger days before he disappeared into his robes and coin. Rebecca hitched herself around the table so she could cast a sideways glance toward the door as I spoke. Sipping her ale as I gulped, watching and watching. I realize now she was hoping not to be seen with me while absorbing my secrets. It did not occur to me that she would use them against me.

When I realized I was pregnant I asked Father Leon for help, daring to expect it. He loved me, was enamored with me, was he not? Instead, he denied knowing me. I had hopes of some advantage for his son to avoid a life of servitude, perhaps even hopes for myself. Surely, he could find a place for me and his child in the church, out of the cold and with a regular meal. I told Rebecca the one secret I should never have told, rolled it drunkenly across the table like dice. My mistake, I see now.

A pebble skitters across the wooden platform. The crowd begins to wander away, finally running out of insults. The aching weight of the iron collar on my shoulders is forcing them to go numb, as my legs are. Sunlight edges behind me, warming the back of my head. Hours to go still. The realization settles over me that I have only just begun my stint on the platform and, as if on cue, my bladder announces itself with great urgency. Perhaps I can kneel to take the strain from my back and allow my bladder to release onto the platform without notice. There is nowhere to hide. However, the chain is hooked to the pillory just high enough to keep me on my feet. There is not enough chain length to allow for a position change, and with that realization, my bladder takes over and releases a flood of hot urine onto my feet. My skirts cover the worst, but the children in the crowd see the spreading puddle and shriek with laughter, then mercifully run away.

Shadows grow below the pillory; the silhouette of my grotesquely caged head spreads across the ground before me. My body numbs and my mind blanks. My head nods as I almost doze, but the spikes of the gag pierce the cuts in the back of my throat, waking me with a sharp stab. Lightheaded. Daggers in my knees. My eyesight is cloudy now, I dare not slump. I strain to catch a glimpse of the figures walking by, still searching for Antony. Villagers gather at the pub. The day is ending, my punishment being the main activity. Evening revelers, barking dogs, sheep in the distance—all merge into a cloud of familiar sound, comforting and distant.

My eyes close involuntarily and my temple finds a resting place on the side of the cage. The sensation of the metal bar, now warm from my heat, lends a false sense of rest for my head. Even the touch of metal is a comfort. The chuck-chuck of a crow's beak pecking stale bread at my feet, bread that crumbled when it bounced off the cage. My spirit floats out above the town, seeking my son, floating toward the dogs and sheep on the outskirts.

I see Rae Ann in my garden. She sits among the feverfew, picking tiny white-and-yellow blossoms, rolling them between her fingers and breathing in their sharp scent. She draws a circle in the soil with her finger and carefully places the flowers in the center, arranging patterns with pebbles. As I watch from above, she steps into the circle, spinning slowly. She seems to be singing, but I cannot hear her voice. My spirit drifts closer to her. She squints upward toward the setting sun, looking right through me. The sound of her name, sharply called, brings us both to attention. Rae Ann stops spinning and her head jerks toward the sound of her mother's voice. Crushed feverfew falls from her hand. Rebecca is coming for her and I am again in the bridle.

Father Leon strides past the pillory toward the refectory, black robes whipping around his ankles. I gaze at his retreating form, remembering his skin beneath my hands, the small dips in his low back just above his hips. But he does not glance my way. I watch his retreat, willing him to see me, but he does not hesitate.

Magistrate appears at my feet, rattling his keys. Boot heels ring out as he ascends the wooden steps. Without a word, he unhooks the chain, inserts the key in the padlock at the back of my neck, scrape of metal on metal. A sharp click and screech as the cage releases from around my head. With no gentleness, he pulls the gag from my mouth, taking bits of tongue and fresh blood along with it. My head lolls on my neck to gain balance and I hear snickers from the few who have gathered for the final scene.

"To the gate," Magistrate orders.

I take a wobbling step and stumble as my legs give way beneath me. My pounding head hangs too heavy to lift and dry throat chokes on its sudden emptiness.

"Right yourself, woman," he commands, eager to be done with me. "To the gate."

He grabs my elbow and hauls me to my feet. I try to ask for my clogs, but my shredded tongue cannot form words and hours without water has left my throat caked with dust and blood. All that emits from my mouth is a sharp rasp.

Magistrate shoves me toward the town gate, such as it is. The stone walls of town have long since crumbled to rubble and the collection of sticks and twine that serve as gates could not prevent entrance to a child, much less reivers. He unlatches the cross branch that secures the rickety panels. The muddy road stretches out before me.

"Get thee gone!"

Banishment

Gates screech closed behind me. I stand on the road outside the village as the last light blinks out between branches of the forest to the west. New stars peek between high, smoky clouds and mournful hooting fills the air. *Where am I supposed to go?* Standing on the road with a mouthful of throbbing tongue remnants, dizzy with fatigue. My throat convulses against the dryness. I haven't had a drink of water in hours, not since this morning. Even so, I have to pee again. This time at least I am free to step off the road and hike my skirts, which I do, focusing to maintain balance.

My cottage is on the outskirts of town where the other mothers of bastards live. I prefer it out there where I am free to grow my garden without the constant peering in of nosy neighbors. They only come to me when they need something—a baby coming or a love potion, a sick chicken or malingering crop. Or a spot of loneliness. I know how to fix these things. If not, I make something up to help them feel better. A tincture or a hex. A string wrapped around wood and bone. A drink of ale or a touch.

If I cut through the sheep pasture around the backside of the village, I might be able to sneak into my cottage and sleep in my own bed one last time. I am sure they will be watching for me, but it is almost pitch black now. I can feel my way around my own cottage in the dark, without a doubt. Perhaps say goodbye to Antony.

I orient myself to the darkness and step further off the road, stumbling on clumps of mud churned by hooves and biting my swollen tongue. Pain shoots through my flesh, reverberating through my scalp, and I flush hot. My nose runs. Late spring chill feels good on my skin. Slow going through field stubble, keeping the village on my right. Soon, I make out the thatch of my roof and see a flicker of firelight beyond—a group of men from the village are in the road, torches alight. I crouch-walk behind my garden wall and peek over the stones. My foot tangles in something soft and I land with an oomph in the dirt.

It's my ragged green cloak tied in a bundle. *Strange.* I burrow my fingers into the loose knot and pull it apart. My clogs! I shove my crusted feet into them. The insides will never be clean again but at least my feet are off the ground. I pull my cloak over my shoulders; its instant, woolen warmth calms the wild thumping of my heart and I see my satchel against the stone wall, as well. I can just make out the shape in the shadows but know its feel like my own skin. *Who left this for me? Antony, perhaps? More likely, Rae Ann. Certainly not Rebecca.* I stoop to pick it up and realize the satchel is full and heavy. Pulling the drawstring open, I find pieces of bread and cheese, and my water jug. My lacerated mouth cannot manage food, but my throat contracts at the thought of a drink of water. I fumble with the cork, then tip the jug back, split lips stinging as they stretch apart. A wash of ale pours into my mouth and down my chin. The jug is full of beer. My mouth is on fire from the alcohol, but I don't care. I gulp and choke, gulp and choke, until the jug is empty. *Gramercy.*

As I watch from behind the crumbled garden wall, the men touch their torches to my thatch roof, their rough faces flashing in the blaze. A shadow shoots past me into the blackberry bramble. Cat. They might hear me if I call her. She won't come anyway. I hunker behind the piles of stones and watch the flames consume the dried thatch of my roof. The searing heat feels good, the snapping sparks cascade like music. I wrap my cloak tightly around my knees and watch flames spread until everything is gone.

The villagers, most of whom I have aided in one way or another over the years, wander away as the blaze dies down, patting each other on the back, as men do. I crawl over the garden wall and curl into the feverfew and mint. Embers glow around the blackened stone walls of my home, radiating heat, and I doze. Sometime in the night, Cat crawls into the cradle between my breast and knees and offers her warmth until morning.

Roosters startle me awake before sunrise and I breathe in the damp smoke of all that remains of my home. My bruised shoulders ache and my mouth is swollen shut. The smoldering ruins of my cottage are no longer warm enough to combat the chill of early dawn. Nothing remains to salvage. A voice calls down the way and I know I will be handed back to Magistrate if I'm seen. I scramble through my own garden in a panic, plucking small sprigs of spring plants from the ground and tucking them into my satchel. *Perhaps I will find a way to start over*, I think, but that thought seems optimistic. Another voice, closer now, and I flee. Behind the garden wall, I run for the tree line, too exposed in the growing light.

Once behind the forest's edge, I lean against rough bark, breathing heavy, rasping through swollen, tattered lips, back aching from my night on the ground and the events of yesterday. I feel a sharp poke in my instep and realize my clogs have flown from my feet and must be scattered in the field. Someone will find them eventually but it is too light to retrieve them now. I cannot risk being discovered. Barefoot it is. I do not know where Antony is. I had hoped he would be somewhere around the cottage. At least he wasn't in the torch-carrying crowd. He is not a child anymore, gone fourteen now. I wonder what he thinks, wonder if he knows I am not actually a heretic. Or a whore. The thought of his accusing eyes from the crowd yesterday, his quick shoulder shrug as he turned on his heel. My chest sinks into my stomach at the memory. Sobs too deep to release flood me. Nothing to do now but go, and so I do.

I know the forest well, its ancient deer paths and knolls. Where the rabbits burrow and the sweet spot where lettuce grows by the spring. Pale silver light glimmers on the forest floor as I head north, away from the village, away from the market road to the next township over. Word will have spread and I am not safe anywhere. *How could I have been so stupid? How could I have not seen this coming?* When Rebecca and I sat in the pub, I saw her sidelong glance to the door every time anyone walked in, like she was looking for a reason to get away from me, but I kept talking. That's what happens when I drink too much. I keep on babbling, long past when I should not. Not only did I tell her Father Leon is Antony's father, I also told her that I leave occasional hexes on his doorstep when I am feeling particularly resentful. Gossiping about myself. *Hoping for what?* As if a shared secret would inspire her loyalty. That's why Magistrate came for me. Blaspheme. *But why did Rebecca betray me? What did she receive in return?* She did not ask for my secrets, but I told them anyway.

Deeper into the forest, the trees obscure sunrise and I pick my way carefully over roots and rocks. Something smacks me on top of the head with enormous force. My knees buckle. I grab the top

of my head, gasping in pain. Had I run into a low-hanging branch?
I stop to look around, my eyes adjusting to the darkness as I
clutch my scalp, panting. Off to the right, a large owl watches me
steadily. *Those were owl talons bashing my skull in.* I stare back for a
moment. *Better to keep moving.*

Hours later, the sun gleams overhead and my stomach growls
with hunger. The faint trail I have been following peters out into
a grotto. I remember this place well—a waterfall tumbles over
boulders into a deep, clear pool. I drop my satchel, shrug off my
cloak, and scramble to the water's edge. I lie on my stomach atop
a flat rock and lean over the pool where the water is still and shallow, intending to scoop a drink. My reflection shimmers back at
me and I am stunned by the stranger on the water's surface. My
hair has gone completely white, gleaming silver under the light
playing on the pool's surface. I relax my body onto the stone, already warm in the sun, and let the heat sink into my belly as I
watch my face hover below. My nose is black and purple and I
trace it with a finger, gasping at the sharp stab of pain. It's broken
and I didn't even realize it, a swollen bump rising in the bridge
and the tip curving sideways above an unrecognizable mouth. A
sallow, green bruise spreads across my cheeks. My lips are bloody
still, the skin split and crusted. My mouth and chin bulge. I gently
touch them and attempt to pry my lips open to see what remains
of my tongue, but I cannot. With trembling hands, I rinse my face
but cannot draw water into my mouth.

I slowly rise from the stone and strip my dress and shift off
over my aching shoulders and peel my rune pouch from where it
sticks to the skin between my breasts. Toss the dress on top of
my cloak on the bank, drop the pouch on top of the dress, and
clamber into the pool with my urine-stained shift clutched in my
hand. I step deeper into the pool, feet finding purchase on the

stony bottom, clear, cold water enveloping my body past my knees, swirling around my thighs, reaching between my legs and over my belly before I stop for a breath. I slowly turn in circles in the deepest valley of the pool, as close as I dare to the falling water, swirling my shift around and around, hoping to relieve it of the stench of urine and sweat. Clouds of bubbles and grime spiral as I spin waist-deep in the pool, around and around. I wring out my slightly cleaner shift, toss it onto the flat rock, and sink under the surface.

Water closes over my head and my white hair strings out through the water like a web, floating upward. The cold feels good on my bruised shoulders and battered face. The water stings the spot where my leather pouch had fused with my skin. The break in the bridge of my nose aches in the frigid water that nevertheless refreshes my swollen lips. I stand, rivulets raining down my breasts. My feet feel their way over the smooth stones and sand. Retrieving my jug from the bank, I return to the waterfall to fill it. There is no easy way to drink—sucking water from my cupped hand proves impossible—but I am able to pour a trickle down my throat from the jug. I cough as the cold water loosens blood clots and scabs, spitting them out into the swirling cascade.

From my vantage in the pool, I see a stand of willows that I had not noticed before and I wade again to the bank. Stepping carefully to avoid blackberry brambles snaking across the ground, I dig my fingernails under the curled edges and strip a piece of bark, and another. A black adder uncoils under a buckthorn shrub and I give it wide berth. Back to the pool to soak the bark, rubbing and rolling it with white pebbles from the shallows to soften it. When the bark is supple enough, I pack small pieces into my cheeks and around my tongue. I form a pillow with my cloak and stretch out on the sun-warmed rock, pressing leaves of carline thistle onto the burning rune mark on my chest where the thrown potato left its imprint.

Afternoon sun prickles my cooled skin and I close my eyes as the willow bark soothes my ravaged mouth and the carline cools my chest. A fat bumblebee hovers near a patch of elderflower, legs heavy with pollen. For a moment, I am enclosed in the purple petals, sunlight shimmering the air to lavender and gold. Purring buzz fills my head, the pull of weights on my legs, heavy, sweet scent lingering. The bumblebee zooms away, frogs sing to their spawn, and I doze in the sun, fingers finding their way to my cunt. Leon is there, young Leon, so certain of his path, the two of us breathless, skin to skin, his kiss on my neck and elsewhere. My hands curve around his shoulders, and I gently flip him onto his back, ensheathing him with a soft chuckle. He gasps and shudders.

I wake, ravenous, peel the macerated bark from my inner cheek, nudge a finger under my tongue to extricate bark fragments from the recesses of swollen tissue and discover an unmoored tooth. And another, then another. I spit the teeth—dead and blue—loosened scabs, and threads of willow bark into the foam of the current. Gently rinse my mouth with a handful of cool water.

The bread and cheese in my satchel have softened in the heat of the afternoon and I tentatively place a pinch of greasy yarg between my remaining teeth. Bit by bit, I coax crumbs down my throat, washed down with sips of spring water. I shake out my damp shift, spread it on the flat rock to dry, and inspect my dress and cloak for damage. Nothing can be done about the dress's ripped hems other than to tear off the tatters. My cloak is missing its clasp, so I retrieve a rowan wood branch from the forest floor, snap it into short lengths, and wrap the twigs with the torn fabric of my dress to make a toggle, tying it all together in a clumsy knot. It's the best I can do.

I will have to venture farther north. If I cannot find a friendly village, I can always return to the grotto. *And do what? Live out my life here?* I have always been a good forager but never lived on wild plants alone. Alone. I have no way to trap meat. No way to cook or start a fire. I might survive the summer in a shelter of fallen branches, but I'll never get through winter on my own. And that's if wolves don't find me first. I have to move on. I turn to pick up my sun-dried shift and discover the adder within it. I fling the shift, adder and all, into the pool with a shriek, my runes scattering through the air, falling like hail into the pool below. Shaking, I pull on my dress and cloak and head north up the rocky slopes toward the sea.

Hut

Days later, I'm not sure how many, a faint trail leads out of the forest and onto limestone ledges under a dappled, rolling sky. Luminous silver clouds release pockets of cold seeping rain that sweep the open bedrock, interspersed with mossy hillocks covered in a thousand glistening streams. Nestled between is a clearing, in which there stands a ring of tall slate stones. The erect stones tower over my head—each facing the others like sentinels—one end rooted in the earth, the other exposed end reaching for the sky. Stones, I figure, that must have been upended by giants. Rhythmic, echoing moans fill my ears as I approach the ring, and I smell smoke. Stumbling closer, I see remnants of charred wood and ash clustered inside the ring at the foot of the tallest stone. I place my hand on its smooth, wet surface and the moaning in my head turns into a deep, howling vibration that seems to come from the stone itself.

Beyond the circle, the towering stones extend in a row toward an opening in a rock ledge, inviting me to shelter. I skirt around the outside of the circle, edge past the forbidding stone queue, and duck into the cave. My eyes cannot adjust to the sudden darkness and my legs give way beneath me. I crawl across the dry cave floor, pebbles imprinting into my palms, skirt dragging in the dust, until I feel a smooth, shallow spot. Dim light from outside makes itself known to me and I curl up in the divot, back against the cold cave wall. Blissful darkness overcomes my mind and I drift, knowing I will not have to endure much longer.

Warmth and a whisper awaken me. My eyes struggle open, lashes tangled together. Hands stroke my arm and bright light fills the opening of the cave. Furs lie beneath and above my body, wrapped like a cocoon.

"Drink this," a voice instructs as a clay cup of something steaming approaches my face, gripped in a gnarled hand with ragged, filth-ringed fingernails. "You're alive," the voice notes. "Drink."

The drink-giver's other hand cradles my head. I find purchase on my elbow and lean toward the cup, slurping its contents into my mangled mouth.

"Ahh, there now. Drink again."

The taste registers somewhere in the crevices of my blistered tongue, nutty and earthy. As the soft warmth of the liquid—*was it tea?*—finds passage down my throat and into my empty belly, a strange tingle spreads through my limbs. The dirty hand offers more.

"Again."

Now that the inside of my mouth and throat are wet, I am able to take in a larger mouthful of the tea. If it is tea.

"Thank you," I attempt to say. The rasping mumble that escapes my mouth is unintelligible, even to me.

"I see you met the scold's bridle," the drink-giver's voice notes as her fingers trace my torn lips.

My eyelids agree to separate from each other, and I look up to see the face of the speaker. I gasp and shiver. *This face. Who has this face?* I reach up to touch her cheekbones protruding beneath sunken sightless eyes clouded with mist. My fingers trace across her scattered silver brows, down deep crevices curving around jutting cheekbones. I run my finger down her hooked beak of a nose and clefted chin. Tears run down my face as she smiles.

"I thought I would never find you," she croons. She sets the tea beside me and nudges me back into the furs, pulling them up over my shoulders. "Stay here. Rest now."

The tea seems to fill my veins with thrumming warmth and I lay back, my arm angled beneath my head as I stare toward the stone circle outside the cave door. Firelight flickers and dances, a wild, alive thing, shimmering vivid pink like wild roses, then blue and green as deep water, and now yellow and orange as poppies and summer fruit. Colors undulate on the cave walls, and I see figures drawn on the stone—cows and bulls, birds and deer—dancing in the flames as if they have come to life and are chasing each other around the cave.

A young woman by the entrance picks cotton fluff from the air. Someone is dancing around the fire ring, too. I see a paunchy beast-man with a hairy chest; a trail of dark, smooth hair descends his round stomach and spreads around his *oh wow, no knickers, here.* He gyrates and spins in the firelight, his tail whipping around behind. *He has a tail. Like a cow's tail with a tuft of hair at the end.* The tea-giver dances wildly beside him, cackling and tossing her long gray hair. I hadn't noticed before, but she isn't wearing any clothes either. I am mesmerized watching the firelight skip over their skin, and take another long draught of tea. The invisible cotton fluffs that the young woman is plucking are actually little shimmering winged things. *Fairies, maybe?* She puts them in her pocket, and they immediately escape and whir back to circle around her head. There are other dancers on the far side of the fire, but I cannot make them out. I hope they dance this way so I can see who or what they are and if they're naked too.

Suddenly, the tea-giver grabs beast-man's tail and throws a leg over it, grasping the tuft between her hands and pulling it back and forth between her legs, head back, howling with laughter. The man does not seem perturbed by this—quite the opposite, he seems to be enjoying it very much. One of the other dancers appears before him, stomping to a beat I hadn't noticed before. The melodies of flute and drum drift in from somewhere out there. The new dancer strokes the round man's member to the music. Somehow, no one falls over. I cannot look away, but my eyes lose focus of their own accord. As I sink into sleep, I could swear the trees beyond the fire ring are swaying in time to the music.

Morning breaks cold and misty, and brings with it a bursting bladder. I struggle reluctantly out of the fur cocoon and stumble to the cave door. Where does one pee in a cave? Toward the back or outside? I opt for outside and step into the fresh air, silent but for birdsong. Tendrils of smoke linger with the early morning mist, but the revelers are gone. Perhaps they are sleeping in the cave. I did not notice. After finding a satisfactory spot behind a bush, I make my way back, longing for my burrow and wondering what might happen next and if there will be breakfast.

At the entrance to the cave, a soft rustling and scraping catches my ear and I turn back toward the stone circle. Emerging from the trees are creatures I have only encountered in childhood tales, approaching me through the ring, their twisted feet dragging across the graveled dirt, peeking around stones. Hunched bodies, stumps where feet should be, gaping, drooling mouths. Bodies draped in scraps of wool and skins; garments strung together with vines. In the middle is the tea-giver, led gently by the girl who caught fairy-flies by the fire.

"Come with us," the tea-giver says.

"Come where?" I ask with quaking voice. "Who are you?"

"I am Síla. These are the outcasts, banished at birth."

The creatures hoot and warble, beckoning me with unnatural fingers. I look down at the monster in front of me. I guess him to be a boy of about ten years old, once I see past his twisted form and into his eyes. And I remember the baby I delivered with malformed limbs. How the terrified father told me it was cursed and to get rid of it, the mother weeping and afraid. "Why, why?" she howled. The husband blamed the mother, the mother blamed me, I blamed the Devil. I left the baby in the woods, swaddled tightly, knowing it was for the best. Can it be he was rescued? *I left others over the years*, I thought, looking around at the outcasts.

The group shifts as one, surrounding me in their midst, herding me on shaking legs toward the trees. My companions move more easily through the woods than they do over stones, hoisting themselves over fallen logs and using trunks as guides. They seem to know the trees individually, which ones mark the path and which ones lead astray.

We come to a clearing in the woods with a pile of logs, which, upon closer inspection, looks to be some sort of hut. Branches and fallen logs leaning against one another form a rudimentary shelter. A rock-ringed firepit in the yard is filled with embers, ash, and clay pots. I see a small stash of precious flint, a pile of firewood, and kindling.

"We keep the fire burning by turns. All are welcome to cook here and keep warm; however, we have our favorite sleeping places in the forest. You are welcome to stay here if you are willing to tend the fire," Síla says.

I nod silently and they turn as one and disappear through the trees, leaving me alone. *They don't trust me.* I clutch my chest, fingers automatically seeking my rune pouch to make sense of this turn of events, but instead I touch the flatness between my breasts and remember my white stones sailing through the air, along with my shift and the black adder, back at the grotto. *They are at the bottom of the waterfall*, I think, rubbing the burning spot between my breasts. Odd that it still hurts. The potato thumping my chest on the pillory, banging against the pouch, and slamming the stones into my breastbone must have been a week ago now, but the spot feels like a fresh burn.

Standing in the silence of the clearing, the outcasts having glided away like so many ghosts, I take stock of my situation. When I peek in a gap between branches—surmising that it reveals the door to the hut—I duck into the hut and see scraps of peeled bark and deer skin woven between the branches, creating remarkably effective protection from the elements. As my eyes adjust to the darkness within, I see a plank shelf against the wall, propped on stones, lined with clay jars. A random assortment of iron tools, or pieces of tools, and an ancient kettle that I can only guess must have been pilfered from travelers or nearby villages. A pile of furs in the corner form a bed.

I squat in front of the display of misshapen clay pots, selecting a few and sniffing their contents. Herbs, seeds, root powders. Mushrooms. Many are empty. None of the lids fit properly. Clay harvested from the bedrock is easy enough to shape into a bowl; however, a smooth finish and fitted lid require skill. There's something to do, at least. I know how to work with seeds and leaves and clay. One empty pot contains a rough lining of crystalline residue. I bring the pot to my nose and sniff deeply. Honey. There are bees around. That is good to know.

The will to live kicks in as I look around the hut. Fill the pots, find the hives, tend the fire. Stay warm and fed. *Strange how figuring out how to stay alive takes over one's mind, even though I am not sure I want to live.* Grief overwhelms me and I set the honey down. Antony will never find me here, even if he cares to look. *What is worse, that he can't find me or that he will not try?* I bury my face in my hands, only to be instantly reminded that my nose is still broken and my mouth tender and swollen from the bridle. I feel a titch of fury behind my eyes and my stomach growls. I do not know how to lay down and die.

I step out to the clearing to stoke the fire and get my bearings. The stone circle is near, just north. The woods are not overly dense and I believe I can avoid getting lost if I leave markers for myself in this unfamiliar landscape. I poke a few pine needles and cones into the embers and place a few small branches over the top. The fire smokes a bit but the pine catches quickly, cones popping loudly. Pine nuts! The pine branches stacked by the hut are loaded with cones and the cones are full of nuts. I pile a thicker branch on top, then retrieve a clay pot from the hut. Pulling branches from the pile I assumed was kindling, and heart pounding, I yank cone after cone from the branches, banging them into the pot, nuts cascading into the bowl. I stop and scoop a handful, pouring them into my mouth without thinking. My few remaining teeth chomp into what is left of my tongue. A scream rises in my throat as my mouth fills with blood, and pain shrieks through my jaw, but I don't dare open my lips because I will lose the pine nuts onto the forest floor. My breath shallow, calming as the pain subsides, I roll the soft nuts between my teeth, gently mashing them and cajoling them down my throat. Fury shakes my pulse.

I need a drink, preferably ale. A stream, not more than a trickle, runs just beyond the stone circle, if I remember rightly. With the largest clay pot in hand, I make my way through the trees, leaving a row of pinecones and bent branches to mark my path back to the hut. At the tree line, the open expanse of valley spreads before me, sun all the way up now, casting cloud shadows across the hillside. I fill the pot at the stream, take a long drink, tongue still smarting. Fill the pot again and take it back to the hut, grateful for my markers. *What now?*

I sit by the firepit, poking the flames. Rage pulses behind my eyes. My stomach rumbles insistently now. There is precious little to make a meal. Best to take to the forest in search of tubers and herbs to add to the mushrooms and pine nuts for a stew. A thought occurs. At the stream, a patch of late spring blooms spreads between the rocks, yellow gorse and primrose. And bees. I have never followed a bee to a hive, since the parish hives were easy pilfering in the village.

I head back to the valley again and squat by the patch of wild-flowers to watch the bees' activities. They come and go. Eventually I discern their direction and follow as closely as I can to a hollow tree just beyond the forest's edge, east of the hut. *I have not thought this through*, I think as I stand before a buzzing hive, realizing my plan has succeeded. My head spins to hold it all. Finding food, making food, tracking directions. All things I have spent a lifetime doing, but always on the perimeter of the village in familiar territory. A quick death at the stake would have been more merciful than slow death by starvation and exposure. The pounding in my head ticks and the rune mark on my chest burns.

I backtrack to the valley and then to the hut to retrieve the kettle. Follow the markers back, collecting sticks along the way. *Where was it now?* Find the bees again, follow again. This time marking the path with bent branches. And, lucky find, a bird car-cass. I grab the desiccated body and tear it wing from vertebrae, threading the pieces on my bent branch markers, white bone making them easier to spot. The skull with its sharp curved beak I thread onto the toggle of my cloak.

Back at the hive, I peek into the tree trunk on tiptoe, where honeycomb glistens just within reach. I drape my cloak over my head for some protection against the likelihood of bee stings. Breathing deeply, evenly, my hand approaches the hive. *Reach. Wait. Slowly, now.* Fingertips touch the wetness of the comb. I can barely see into the hollow, but my fingers find their way, grasping the honeycomb and sinking into the cells, honey oozing between them. I hold my breath, expecting to be stung. Gently pull, extracting a large piece of dripping honeycomb. I take a bite, saliva spurting into the corners of my crusted lips. Sticky sweetness slides down my throat and chin, and I take another bite, then another, ravenous, until nothing is left. I reach into my bodice and rub my honey-coated fingers into the burning rune mark, skin instantly soothed. The bees seem to accept my presence, crawling lightly over my arms. I lick my fingers. Deep breath, one more reach into the tree. Extract another piece, larger than the first, and drop it into the kettle. One more and one more. I thank the bees silently and ease away.

Back to the markers along the path, stopping only to yank a handful of angelica root. I must look like a mad woman, raven skull at my throat, bees clinging to my white hair, cloak bundled full of roots, herbs, and rattling seed pods. Rusted kettle full of honeycomb in the crook of my arm, face likely purple with bruises, nose warped and bent. The realization that in order to stay alive I must do this every day for the rest of my life—which likely will not be long—ignites the pulse behind my eyes.

I arrive back at the hut, exhausted and furious. Drop my gatherings beside the fire, which needs stoking again. I am grateful for the hut and the fire, to be sure, but the temptation lurks to wander off over the heather and let the vultures take me. The pounding in my head increases as I rekindle the flames, rinse the roots, break them into pieces, put them in the kettle with the honeycomb. Belly growling again, reminding me that a few mouthfuls of honeycomb after days of nothing is not enough. My fear is wearing down and the hunger is rising. I head into the hut to peruse the clay pots, finding aniseed and sweet flag. Into the kettle they go, along with the pine nuts. I pile dried branches onto the fire, which bloom into crackling sparks that quickly die out. Frustrated and starving, exhausted from walking since sunup—and days before that—my mind fogs over. I grab the long barkstripped stick I used to cajole the embers and begin beating the fire, enraged. Sparks fly. The branches burst into flames. I stop, panting heavily, my pulse and headache pounding in my busted nose.

I settle the kettle into the flames, stirring the concoction with my ash- and pitch-covered stick. Stabbing the honeycomb, mashing roots, seeds, and herbs against the side of the pot, I pulverize the mixture into a glistening, burbling mass. I watch the yellow and golden potion churn, scraping the bottom of the kettle, turning the speckles of root, nuts, and seeds, over and over. As I stir the pynade, always Rae Ann's favorite, the sweet coalesces and images form in the undulating mass.

The face of Rebecca appears, but not the Rebecca who sneers and prickles. She is concentrating, the soft *whir, whir, whir* of her spindle creating rhythm. She has that little crease between her eyebrows like she always does when her thoughts dissect from her hands.

A cat, my cat, wraps around her ankles and slinks for the next room, and I see what Cat sees. Rae Ann at the hearth, prodding embers with a poker, contemplating the glowing flames. Cat settles beside her feet, ears at attention. Rae Ann's head tilts as she hears the door creak open in the other room, and footsteps enter, unannounced.

Her mother's spindle stops whirring, stool scrapes floor, clothing rustles. Rae Ann holds the poker still to listen.

"Father Leon. Please stop, Father."

"Hush. Submit to me."

"I cannot feed another child if you won't help me feed this one. Surely, you must tire of me."

Father Leon laughs.

"You must provide some assistance," she insists. "Did you bring some firewood at least? Some coin?"

"I cannot bring you charities, Rebecca, for all the town to see. Do you want to be seen as a beggar? If so, come to the church and ask like the rest. Besides, a missed meal or two will keep your waist trim. Why do I continue to return to you? Perhaps you're casting hexes on me? Hmm."

"What are you talking about?"

"There is witchery here. I know it. Only a witch would tempt me the way that you do. What are these roots in your basket?"

Rae Ann hears her mother's basket roll across the floor.

"They're from Delfa."

"No wonder you stink of magic. She is the lowest of harlots and if you abide by her, you'll be tainted. Her lustful nature and love of ale is of the Devil. Be careful of consorting with such a woman, lest you be outcast, as well."

"How dare you threaten me. I'll tell the village Antony is yours, I swear I will. Delfa told me. I see the way you look at her, despite your warnings. How many children in the village are yours? How dare you leave us all to starve in the shadow of the cross."

Rebecca's body collides with the wall. Rae Ann grips the poker, knuckles white. Cat leaps lightly to her shoulder. The three of us together stare around the corner.

"That's blaspheme, you whore." Leon wraps his hand around Rebecca's throat and squeezes. "Everyone knows Delfa's child could be anyone's. For all I know that boy could be the spawn of the Devil himself. Spreading lies about her holy father is heresy. You will keep your mouth shut or be accused of the same. Or worse," Father Leon hisses as his grip tightens around Rebecca's throat. "The scripture demands thou shalt not suffer a witch to live and, witch or not, the bridle waits for Delfa's loose tongue. Hold your tongue or I'll have you put in the bridle as well, or perhaps the bootes. Have you seen the bootes, Rebecca?"

Rebecca, eyes wide, shakes her head against the spread of his thick fingers.

I watch as Leon heaves Rebecca onto the bed in the corner and climbs on beside her, hand gripping a handful of her hair. He grabs her calf with his other hand and pulls it toward her belly. "The bootes, Rebecca, encompass your lovely shins in oak planks held together by iron screws." Father Leon smiles and kisses her knee. "With each denial of your sins, the screws tighten. Should a witch refuse to confess, it is safe to say she will never walk again by the time Magistrate is finished with her."

Father Leon chuckles and releases Rebecca's leg. He rolls over on top of her and growls, "You will confess to Magistrate that Delfa spread blaspheme and heresy about her holy father. You will tell him today or I'll have you arrested for witchcraft and then we shall see how you like being a crippled beggar. Perhaps then you will receive the charity you feel you deserve and I will have Rae Ann in my bed by nightfall."

Father Leon releases Rebecca and stalks to the door, adjusting his robe. He sees Rae Ann watching and stops to meet her gaze. His eyes scour her body. I can feel Rae Ann tremble as he swirls out and Rebecca sobs on the bed.

"Mama," Rae Ann whispers.

Rebecca doesn't answer.

"Run, Rae Ann," I whisper. "Fly, my child."

The pynade is ready, bubbling wildly, a deep amber now. I have not prepared a place to spread it out. Of course I haven't. I haul the kettle from the flames, run into the hut to retrieve the plank shelf, slap it down onto a stump, and give it a cursory wipe with my hem to clear it of dust. I pick up the kettle, not feeling the hot metal in my hands, and pour the scalding brew slowly onto the plank. The candy spreads to the edges of the wood, its heavy scent of spiced molten honey filling my nose. I watch it settle and harden, tilting the wooden tray to keep the confection centered, nipping off sticky edges as they cool and sucking them with my tattered tongue.

Rae Ann

Rae Ann slips out the door, Cat at her feet, and runs down the road toward the outskirts of town. She scrambles over Delfa's garden wall and into her hut, throwing food and a jug into a satchel, grabbing whatever she can find. She dumps the armload behind the stone wall, meaning to come back for it.

"What are you doing here, Rae Ann?" Antony asks. "Why are you always in our garden?"

Rae Ann whips around. "Nothing, just looking for your mum. Is she here?"

"No, she's in the woods, as usual. Why?"

Rae Ann stands stock-still staring at Antony's face.

"What is wrong with you? Get out of here, Rae Ann."

Rae Ann turns toward home. Standing in the street, she sees Rebecca walking slowly toward Magistrate's office. Rae Ann turns to see Delfa emerge from the tree line, her basket overflowing with greens, herbs, and flowers. Rae Ann falls to her knees.

Rebecca

Leather straps bind my torso to a tall wooden chair, my arms and my legs trapped in iron plates, the dank, musty air of the dungeon in my nostrils.

Magistrate stands before me, spinning his cane in the sliver of light from one high window. He paces back and forth. "Livestock falling down dead, a stillbirth. An entire family smitten with uncontrollable vomiting and shites. It seems we have witches among us—still."

He clicks his heels on the stone floor. "What say you?"

I watch him pace, mouth agape, uncertain what to say. Since Delfa's banishment, the air in the village seems alive like a beating heart. It is true that many strange things are happening, but they have nothing to do with me.

Our Father who art in Heaven.

"The villagers are frightened, seeing a witch behind every tree and a Devil in every flame."

I stare at Magistrate, comprehension settling on me, swallowing against my dry throat. Just this morning, I swear I heard whispers fall silent as I walked by a cluster of women trading wares. I smiled and greeted them, and saw their faces turn still as

I passed. Once a few paces away, their conversations resumed. Everyone knows I confessed to Delfa's heresy and got her banished. I had no choice. It didn't help that the men burned Delfa's cottage to the ground and her boy is missing. Tensions are running high, but it's not my fault.

Hallowed be Thy name.

Magistrate smirks, tapping his cane onto the floor. "There must be witches responsible for this high strangeness, no? Are you a witch, Rebecca?"

"No," I say, meeting his gaze.

"No?" he murmurs. "Are you certain?"

"Yes, I'm certain," I answer. Of course, I am certain. I'm not a witch.

Thy Kingdom come. Thy will be done.

"Hmmm . . ." Magistrate trades his cane for a pair of iron pincers from a table in the corner. He puts his left hand on top of my right, smashing my palm to the arm of the chair. The cold sting of iron pokes the tip of my first finger, the pincers grip my fingernail. He pulls with a ferocity I did not anticipate. My fingernail rips from my flesh, the whole of it, blood seeping around the nail bed. I scream.

"Do you consort with the Devil?"

"No."

On earth as it is in Heaven.

"No?"

Another nail.

"Did you cast a spell of perversion upon Father Leon?"

"NO!"

Another nail.

"Do you kill children? Do you eat them?"

"Nooooooo . . ."

Give us this day, our daily bread.

Another nail.

My arm is convulsing against the straps, my guts churn, and my throat gags. Blood from my fingertips leaks everywhere. Whole fingernails on the floor. Each new rip raw and screaming.

And forgive us our trespasses as we forgive those who trespass against us. Lead us not into temptation.

My sight blurs as the Magistrate positions the pincers on my thumb.

"Are you a witch, Rebecca?" he implores as his grip tightens.

"Yes," I scream.

But deliver us from evil.

"Yes," I hear myself sob. "Yes, yes."

"Ah."

I take a shaking breath as he lowers the pincers. My bleeding fingers curl against themselves.

"And who joins you?" he purrs.

"Who-who, what?" I gasp for air.

"Who are your fellow consorts, your witch-sisters?" he urges, banging the pincers against the back of my hand.

"No, no one. Just, just me," I stammer.

"Cannot be. I demand to know who joins your decadence, your Devil worship," he says. *"Who is in your coven!?"*

My head hangs to my chest. I cannot see through the pain as the iron pincers again collide with my fractured hand. *Who? Who can I name?*

Magistrate lays the pincers on the floor and tightens the bolts of the leg press, the bootes, first my right leg, then my left. *Squeeze.* I remember Father Leon's description of me as a crippled beggar, sitting in rags by the church door. *Tighter now.* Pain shoots up my legs into my pelvis. My feet swell with blood and a hot gush of urine soaks my skirt.

"Name her!"

My pain-scrambled mind makes a decision. *Delfa.* She is already banished. What more can they do to her? If I know my sister, they will never find her. *I hope.*

For Thine is the Kingdom, the power, the glory. Forever and ever.

The flesh of my calf is caught between the boote planks, pinched through the skin. He tightens the bolts. Something in my leg makes a cracking sound.

"Delfa," I whisper.

Rae Ann

I can't find anyone. Mama was taken to the courthouse yesterday and never came back. I think maybe she is dead. Delfa was banished a week ago now. Antony is gone and I can't find Cat. I hear Delfa's voice in my head saying *fly, fly, fly*, and I keep smelling honey but I can't fly. I am not a bird. And I'm hungry. I eat the last of our bread as I walk to Delfa's garden. I will gather her cloak that I hid behind the garden wall and try to find her. I bet she went to the grotto. I have never walked that far into the forest by myself, but I think I can do it.

I get to the garden wall behind Delfa's burned-down house. The cloak is gone, so is her satchel. I stomp through the feverfew patch looking for the bundle I know I left there and hear horses coming down the road. Lots of horses. I hunker down in the bushes and see Magistrate and Father Leon thunder by on horseback, followed by others.

I am too late.

Delfa

The fire is out. Evening chill approaches quickly and I must re-kindle the flames before dark. Panic engulfs my mind and I cannot remember how to spark flint. Perhaps Síla can help me if I can find her. I run to the stone circle, hoping she will be there. I stumble to the middle of the ring, turning around and around, calling her name, my voice on the edge of hysteria. No answer. *The cave, maybe she is in the cave,* I think, staggering toward the opening, and then I see her above the entrance, embedded in the rock ledge. Her wide, sightless eyes carved in stone, bared teeth above emaciated ribcage, dilapidated breasts hanging to her navel. Her bent knees are spread apart and her long, thin fingers emerge from behind her calves to hold open her pudenda. I cannot reach her. Síla has been turned to stone. Or was she a dream from the start?

I hear the clatter of horses' hooves and freeze.

Before I can run, thundering hooves carrying Magistrate burst into the clearing. He peers down at me from the horse's back with a familiar sneer. Behind him, another horse arrives holding Father Leon—who seems to be hanging on for dear life—followed by a group of men on horseback. Men I do not know but who look young and strong. Magistrate and Father Leon dismount in a swirl of pompous cloakery.

Magistrate strides forward, cracking his horsewhip on the ground. "Delfa Cameron, kneel!" he commands.

My mind goes blank and my knees involuntarily give way. He stops in front me, eyes blazing from above.

"We know you returned to the village to exact your revenge in the form of witchcraft. Your feeble attempts to cast spells as retaliation for your well-deserved punishment brings the wrath of our Lord Jesus Christ upon you. Your sister, Rebecca Cameron, has named you as the Devil's consort."

Magistrate paces before me, swirling on his heel, nodding to the men on horseback, one of whom slides to the ground, pulling a bundle from the back of his horse and across his shoulder. He steps forward and drops the bundle at Magistrate's feet. It is the body of Rebecca.

Magistrate returns his attention to me, his eyes burning like embers. "As we pursued you, we found that evidence of your sorcery abounds. Your clogs were found in the field with your strangled familiar. The spring in the grotto churns your shift without you in it. Frog spawn and black adder entrails strung on bramble thorns on the creek bank. A ring of stones carved with hexes. Proof of your black magic! You have chosen to pursue wickedness against the very village that was your home and against Christ Himself. Your punishment—as was your sister's—is death."

He forces my arms behind my back and ties a rope around my wrists, then steps up onto an outcrop of stone, pulling upward on the rope until only my toes brush the ground and my head hangs to my knees. Muscles in my shoulders wrench and shriek. Blood rushes to my face, pulsing in my broken nose.

Magistrate barks an order and the men on horseback dismount, scrambling to obey. He directs them to build a fire within the stone circle.

"Just there, where the ashes lie." His command comes out in a slightly breathless warble as he strains to hold me aloft.

My arms are detaching from my shoulders. My mind is strangely calm as it notes this new situation in which my body finds itself.

Father Leon inches behind his horse. The men scurry to gather logs and lay a crosshatch of fallen branches at the base of the tallest stone.

Magistrate steps down and I collapse at his feet. He yanks the rope. "On your feet, witch!"

The butt of his cane knocks between my shoulder blades as he shoves me forward, making me march ahead of him up the aisle of stones toward the bier. He is careful not to touch me if he can help it, keeping a cane's length distance between us. I am convinced he loves nothing more than having a woman at the end of a leash. His excitement is palpable. Stone sentinels loom above, their striated gray surfaces exude hollow, vibrating echoes in the chill evening air.

"Father Leon, should we show Delfa the mercy of strangulation? Or shall she feel the lick of flames on flesh to prepare for her final destination?" Magistrate questions.

"It matters not to me, Magistrate," Father Leon squeaks, his voice far different from its ordinary rumble.

"Flames it is, then, Father," Magistrate concedes.

He loops the rope around the stone and brings it back around my torso, lashing my body to the monolith, his breath like rot against my skin. I cannot breathe from fury. Prickling rope fibers dig through my clothing into my skin and itch. Cold slate unyielding against my back, my arms disjointed and limp. The towering circle of stones emits a pulsating roar, a menacing, excited canticle, and I wonder if anyone else can hear it.

I watch Father Leon's face. *Does he remember? Will he save me?* Father Leon looks away and nods to Magistrate, whose face fills my vision as he lights the fire.

Disquiet in the Realm

Sizzling pops burn my ears and smoke fills my nose and blinds my eyes. I breathe deep, pulling fumes into my lungs, exhaling a cloud of vapor. From above, I see my body below, surrounded by flames within the ring of stones. My head lolls on my shoulder above my limp body. Empty eyes gaze without sight as flames lick the fibers of my cloak. Silver stones reflect the flicker and glow of firelight as tongues of flame catch all at once. On fire, my ragged skirts billow and screech. Clouds of heat scorch my face; black smoke swirls and rises to my hoverance like a vulture circling above as flames catch flesh. Coils of smoke separate into tiny winged vibrations, moving in unison with the current of shimmering heat, swarming around the flames and my burning skin. Thrumming intensifies as fire encompasses my breasts, my shoulders, my head. Sparks whorl in unison with swarms of bees. Flames sizzle my hair; curls alight curdling like snakes. Raven skull at my throat screeches. Mangled lips and tongue blaze to life and my skull emerges suddenly through the fire, smooth and burnished as copper. Eye sockets fill with flames that stretch and reach for Magistrate and Father Leon. As the two cower before the pinnacle of my flaming flesh, clouds of black smoke, flames, and swarms of bees erupt from my eye sockets and circle the men huddled in their robes. Their screams fill the air but fade quickly. They are soon overcome and vanish in the toxic cloud. My skull detaches from my spine and rolls to the foot of the stone pillar as the last tendrils of acrid smoke buoy me upward, toward cool air currents far above.

Floating to the north and west above moonlit landscape, over silver caps and silent darkness of the sea, a glow in the distance beckons. Light emanates from another circle of stones, their edges worn by the wind and rain of a million years. This circle is like the other, but older. Softer somehow. The stones are mossy, worn smooth, and tucked gently into the landscape. Closer now. Full moon hovers directly above, stones reach upward like waiting arms. I pull back into the draft, which eddies around me like water, offering resistance. I rise to see the glimmer and pulse of the ground within the circle of stones. The air within radiates green and gold. *Are the hills holding up the stones or are the stones holding the hills in place? Are the stones holding up the moon or is the moon pulling up the stones?* Faint drumbeats and soft chanting fill the air. I cannot make out the words or even tell where the sounds are coming from.

The air beneath me hovers over the stone circle and begins to settle. I gently descend onto shimmering earth. Nagging thoughts—pinpricks—of *how am I doing this without a body* fracture and waft away. I lie on mounds of moss, warm and soft as velvet. Fragrance of earth and salt, tangy and sweet. Glare of the moon a magnetic pull holding me in place, the weight of its light like a stone on my chest. Drumbeats flow from the stones looming above, chanting seeps up from the ground like water after heavy rain. Drumbeats and chants merge into song and light, swelling, filling, pulsating the air. *The air is singing.* I close my eyes and I rest.

Shimmering waves of light, green and blue
Hovering over the sea
Fade as light rises in the east
Stones turn to silver at moonset
I stretch along the shore between night and day
Rising and falling with the waves
Mother calls from the receding darkness
Where are you, little one? Come now
I follow her rhythmic chanting
Light follows me, washing deep blue to white and gold
Follow her voice
Seeking shelter in her deepness
She is always a step ahead
A tempest unseen, a trail of unrest
Always out of sight
Just beyond the horizon

Acknowledgments

Boundless gratitude to:

Friends and family who read my shitty first drafts even when they didn't want to.

Anneliese Kamola for developmental editing and for your understanding and encouragement.

Ken Miller for cover art that captured the soul of this book.

Lisa Dailey and the whole Sidekick Press team for bringing this book to life. It's better than I imagined.

Most of all to Steve who supported me in every way throughout this whole process. You are the love of my life. Thank you for letting me follow my path.

Resources

Part 1

A&E. *Mary Kay Letourneau: Autobiography*. Accessed January 4, 2023. https://play.aetv.com/specials/mary-kay-letourneau-autobiography /full-special.

Hitt, Tarpley. "The Mystical Megachurch Ruling over Megan Rapinoe's Hometown." The Daily Beast, July 25, 2019, https://www.thedailybeast.com/the-mystical-megachurch-ruling-over-world-cup-soccer-star-megan-rapinoes-hometown.

Kriel, Charles, director. *People You May Know*. Metrotone Media, September 28, 2020. https://www.imdb.com/title/tt12606876/.

Nelson, Anne. *Shadow Network: Media, Money, and the Secret Hub of the Radical Right*. Bloomsbury Publishing, 2021.

Russell, Ronna. *The Uncomfortable Confessions of a Preacher's Kid*. Black Rose Writing, 2019.

Part 2

"Magic to Poisonous: Avoid These 6 Idaho Mushrooms at All Costs." 103.5 KISSFM, April 11, 2022. https://1035kissfmboise.com/magic-to-poisonous-avoid-these-6-idaho-mushrooms-at-all-costs/.

"The Cuyamaca Water Company Partnership: New Scenes from San Diego's Water History." San Diego History Center, November 4, 2016. https://sandiegohistory.org/journal/2016/april/cuyamaca-water-company-partnership-new-scenes-san-diegos-water-history/.

"Use Caution When Foraging for Wild Plants, Mushrooms." Idaho Fish and Game, May 11, 2020. https://idfg.idaho.gov/press/use-caution-when-foraging-wild-plants-mushrooms.

Digital Atlas of Idaho: 122. https://digitalatlas.cose.isu.edu/geog/rrt/part5 /122.htm.

Hillman, Bill and Sue-On Hillman. "Historical Photos of Pocatello." ERBzine 3657a. https://www.erbzine.com/mag36/3657a.html.

Kerber, Linda K., et al. *Women's America: Refocusing the Past*. Oxford University Press, 2020.

Matthews, Mychel. "Hidden History: Trouble over Water Supply Ends in Riot." *Twin Falls Times-News*, November 18, 2021, https://magicvalley.com/news/local/hidden-history-trouble-over-water-supply-ends-in-riot/article_8a75d4e7-11c4-5e71-9e37-7f9d31aac179.html.

Parry, Darren. *The Bear River Massacre: a Shoshone History*. Common Consent Press, 2019.

Skaggs, Jackie Johnson. "History of Pocatello, Bannock County, Idaho." Idaho Genealogy, May 8, 2019. https://idahogenealogy.com/bannock/history_pocatello_bannock_county.htm.

Smith, Justin. "A Well-Preserved View of Pocatello's Early Days." *Idaho State Journal*, December 20, 2019, https://www.idahostatejournal.com/opinion/columns/a-well-preserved-view-of-pocatellos-early-days/article_b157523a-1ac3-5a88-8962-cb4a7a01ffe9.html.

Wrigley, Robert L., Jr. "The Early History of Pocatello, Idaho." *The Pacific Northwest Quarterly*, Vol. 34, No. 4 (Oct. 1943): 353–365. https://www.jstor.org/stable/40486626

Part 3

Anon, Anon S. "Sexual Relations between Elite White Women and Enslaved Men in the Antebellum South: A Socio-Historical Analysis." *Inquiries Journal*, August 1, 2013. http://www.inquiriesjournal.com/articles/1674/sexual-relations-between-elite-white-women-and-enslaved-men-in-the-antebellum-south-a-socio-historical-analysis.

Davidson, James M. "Deconstructing the Myth of the 'Hand Charm': Mundane Clothing Fasteners and Their Curious Transformations into Supernatural Objects." *Historical Archaeology* 48, no. 2 (2014): 18–60. JSTOR, http://www.jstor.org/stable/43491391.

Eble, Connie. "Creole in Louisiana." *South Atlantic Review* 73, no. 2 (2008): 39–53. JSTOR, http://www.jstor.org/stable/27784777.

Hodes, Martha. *White Women, Black Men: Illicit Sex in the 19th Century South*. Yale University Vail-Ballou Press, 1997.

Johnson, Elizabeth Ofosuah. "The Disturbing History of Enslaved Mothers Forced to Breastfeed White Babies in the 1600s." *Face2Face Africa*, August 20, 2018. https://face2faceafrica.com/article/the-disturbing-history-of-enslaved-mothers-forced-to-breastfeed-white-babies-in-the-1600s.

Jones-Rogers, Stephanie E. *They Were Her Property: White Women as Slave Owners in the American South*. Yale University Press, 2020.

PBS. "Olaudah Equiano." *Africans in America, Part 1*. https://www.pbs.org/wgbh/aia/part1/1p276.html.

PBS. "Slave with Iron Muzzle." *Africans in America, Part 1*. https://www.pbs.org/wgbh/aia/part1/1h308.html.

Ward, Beth. "The Long Tradition of Folk Healing among Southern Appalachian Women." Atlas Obscura, November 27, 2017.

https://www.atlasobscura.com/articles/southern-appalachia-folk-healers-granny-women-neighbor-ladies.

Part 4

"'Such Was the Tumultation These Women Made': The Women of Marblehead Wreak Revenge upon Indian Captors, 1677." History Matters—The U.S. Survey Course on the Web. http://historymatters.gmu.edu/d/5835/.

Baker, Emerson W. *Storm of Witchcraft.* Oxford University Press, 2016.

Blankfield, Bryan. "The Gustatory Ethics of 'Consider the Lobster.'" *Animals, Food, and Tourism,* 2018, pp. 12–21. https://doi.org/10.4324/9781315265209-2.

Kamensky, Jane. *The Colonial Mosaic: American Women, 1600–1760.* Oxford University Press, 1998.

Speare, Elizabeth George. *The Witch of Blackbird Pond: And Related Readings.* Clearinghouse for Specialized Media & Technology, 2003.

Part 5

"18th Century Scottish Folk Medicine." Burns Birthplace Blog, September 11, 2017. https://burnsmuseum.wordpress.com/2017/09/11/18th-century-scottish-folk-medicine/.

"Foraging." *NatureScot.* https://www.nature.scot/professional-advice/social-and-economic-benefits-nature/food-and-drink/foraging.

"History of Scotland's Woodlands." *NatureScot.* https://www.nature.scot/professional-advice/land-and-sea-management/managing-land/forests-and-woodlands/history-scotlands-woodlands.

"Puiteachen Cottage." Forestry and Land Scotland. https://forestryandland.gov.scot/learn/heritage/historic-woodland-use/puiteachen.

Boose, Lynda E. "Scolding Brides and Bridling Scolds: Taming the Woman's Unruly Member." *Shakespeare Quarterly* 42, no. 2 (1991): 179. https://doi.org/10.2307/2870547.

Estés, Clarissa Pinkola. *Women Who Run with the Wolves.* Rider, 2022.

Federici, Silvia. *Witches, Witch-Hunting, and Women.* PM Press, 2018.

Frances Jenkins Olcott. "The Witch-Cat." FairyTalez, April 18, 2021, https://fairytalez.com/the-witch-cat/.

Kors, Alan Charles, and Edward Peters. *Witchcraft in Europe, 400–1700: A Documentary History.* University of Pennsylvania Press, 2001.

Levack, Brian P. *The Witch-Hunt in Early Modern Europe.* Routledge, Taylor & Francis Group, 2016.

MacCulloch, Canon J. A. "The Mingling of Fairy and Witch Beliefs in Sixteenth and Seventeenth Century Scotland." *Folklore* 32, no. 4 (1921): 227–44. http://www.jstor.org/stable/1255201.

Sellin, Thorsten, and William Andrews. "Bygone Punishments." *Journal of Criminal Law and Criminology (1931–1951)* 22, no. 6 (1932): 941. https://doi.org/10.2307/1136221.

Simpson, Jacqueline. "'The Weird Sisters Wandering': Burlesque Witchery in Montgomerie's 'Flyting.'" *Folklore* 106 (1995):9–20. http://www.jstor.org/stable/1260748.

About the Author

Photo by Steve Mitchell

Ronna Russell is a published author and a recent university graduate. After raising a family and divorcing, she moved from the Pacific Northwest to Ohio, remarried, published a memoir (*The Uncomfortable Confessions of a Preacher's Kid*), and enrolled at Kent State University, graduating in December 2022 at the age of fifty-six with a Bachelor of Integrative Studies in Creative Writing, Women's Studies, and Anthropology. *Scold's Bridle* began during Ronna's time at the university. She is a neurodivergent pagan, writer, scrap artist, and visual thinker.

Printed in the USA
CPSIA information can be obtained
at www.ICGtesting.com
CBHW060109060524
7981CB00006B/23